Monotheism

The Identity of God

Sayed Moustafa Al-Qazwini, PhD

Monotheism: The Identity of God
Sayed Moustafa Al-Qazwini, PhD

First Published in 2022 by
Islamic Educational Center of Orange County
3194-B Airport Loop Drive
Costa Mesa, California, 92626
Tel: (714) 432-0060

Website: **www.iecoc.org**
E-mail: **info@iecoc.org**

IECOC
@IECOC
@IECOC

ISBN 978-0-99-890551-8

Cover Design and Layout by Islamic Publishing House (www.iph.ca)

Contents

The Chapter of Sincerity[1]

بِسْمِ ٱللَّهِ ٱلرَّحْمَٰنِ ٱلرَّحِيمِ

In the Name of God, the All-Compassionate, the All-Merciful

قُلْ هُوَ ٱللَّهُ أَحَدٌ

Say: "He, God, is One,

ٱللَّهُ ٱلصَّمَدُ

God, the Eternally Sufficient unto Himself.

لَمْ يَلِدْ وَلَمْ يُولَدْ

He begets not; nor was He begotten,

وَلَمْ يَكُن لَّهُۥ كُفُوًا أَحَدٌ

And none is like unto Him."

---

[1] Qur'an, Surah al-Ikhlaas (112), verses 1-5.

Preface

بِسۡمِ ٱللَّهِ ٱلرَّحۡمَٰنِ ٱلرَّحِيمِ

In the Name of God, the All-Compassionate, the All-Merciful.

The last few decades has seen the emergence of an intensified version of the debate regarding the existence of God, His identity, as well as the significance of belief in Him as an Almighty Being.

Surely, through reaching the pinnacle of scientific and technological advancement, some have argued that the belief in a higher power has been made redundant; for man is able to explain many natural phenomenon, while simultaneously being able to provide an adequate solution to some of them, therefore, evidently religion is merely a matter of history.

On the other hand, monotheists and people who believe in the existence and power of God have many questions on their mind. Amongst them are: Why does a Merciful and Wise God allow suffering to take place on Earth? Why does such a God allow poverty, pandemics, oppression, and injustice to take over? If God is truly - as the monotheists suggest - Omnipotent, Omnipresent, and Omniscient, then why do we not see any intervention from Him to stop the crimes, corruption, and all of the misery that is rampant throughout the world?

These questions, and others, prompted me to introduce the theme of monotheism and its branches to the readers, in a simple and concise way. The complex philosophical and theological discussions which have taken place in this arena have been omitted due to the lack of interest that most people have in them.

Monotheism is the knowledge of recognizing God, discovering Him, and discovering His identity. How does He present Himself throughout the verses of the Qur'an, and how can His servants reach out to Him? Monotheism is the first step to understanding religion. Without understanding it, the intricate details of religion will be incomprehensible. Understanding God is the key to understanding His messengers, apostles, scriptures, Divine Justice, the Day of Judgment, and ultimately, our journey in this life.

To enhance this discussion on understanding God, in addition to the differences between monotheism and polytheism, I tried to use Qur'anic verses as much as possible throughout. My intention was to create a brief, yet essential, introduction to understanding the theme of monotheism and its branches.

This work could not have been accomplished without the help of Sister Malihe Elias, who wrote the initial inscription, and Sister Jolanda Hendriks, who organized the text; may God reward them both abundantly.

I must also express my gratitude to my honorable friend, Shaykh Saleem Bhimji, for reviewing and publishing this book; and his wife, Sister Arifa Hudda for editing the contents; and a benevolent personality, who prefers to remain anonymous, for their generous donation towards the publication of this book.

Finally, I extend my gratitude to my family, who helped and supported me in putting this work together. I ask God for guidance so that I can present the truth, and to protect me from any kind of intellectual or spiritual deviation.

وَمَا تَوْفِيقِيٓ إِلَّا بِٱللَّهِۚ عَلَيْهِ تَوَكَّلْتُ وَإِلَيْهِ أُنِيبُ

> And my success lies with God alone. In Him do I trust, and unto Him will I return.[1]

Sayed Moustafa Al-Qazwini
Jamadi al-Akhir 21st, 1443 AH
January 25th, 2022 CE
Los Angeles, California

---

[1] Qur'an, Surah Hud (11), verse 88.

Introduction

All praise is due to our Lord, the Cherisher, the Sustainer, and the Provider. May His peace and blessings be upon all of His messengers and His apostles: those who came to teach and guide us to the right path - the path of success, prosperity, and salvation. May His peace and blessings be upon the seal of the Messengers, Prophet Muhammad, and his pure and immaculate family, and his righteous companions.

This book is based on a Ramaḍan 1436 AH / 2015 CE Ahlulbayt TV month-long series entitled *Enquiries about Allah*, which can be found on YouTube and on https://www.al-islam.org/.

Qur'an translations have been adopted from *The Study Qur'an*[1] with some paraphrasing.

At times, the Arabic terms have been included to maintain the accurate meaning of certain sentences.

It is customary in Islam that when the name of God, Prophet Muhammad, the other prophets, or Imams (descendants and successors of Prophet Muhammad) are expressed, the following phrases are mentioned:

Allah/God - Glorified and Exalted is He
(*Subhannaho wa-ta'ala*)
Written abbreviation - SWT

Prophet Muhammad - Peace be upon him and his family
(*sallallahu alayhi wa alehi wasallam*)
Written abbreviation - pbuh & hf

---

[1] *The Study Qur'an: A New Translation and Commentary.* 2015. Edited by Seyyed Hossein Nasr. Published by HarperOne.

After the names of the other prophets, Imams from the family of Prophet Muhammad, and his daughter - Peace be upon him/her
(*alayhi/a salaam*)
Written abbreviation - pbuh

With great respect, admiration, acknowledgment, and praise, I have omitted the mentioned phrases for the sake of continuity. In addition, I have capitalized the term "Imam(s)" when referring to the twelve Imams of the *Ahlulbayt*.

1

Significance of Monotheism

وَلَقَدْ بَعَثْنَا فِي كُلِّ أُمَّةٍ رَّسُولًا أَنِ ٱعْبُدُوا۟ ٱللَّهَ وَٱجْتَنِبُوا۟ ٱلطَّٰغُوتَ

> Indeed, to every community, we sent a messenger (saying): "Worship God and shun false deities."[1]

[1] Qur'an, Surah al-Nahl (16), verse 36.

The theme of monotheism, since the creation of man on earth, has been the foundation of all Divine messages. Every messenger of God began his mission first by inviting people to embrace the belief in God and His Sovereignty. Monotheism is the core value of Islam and the prime essence of its message.

The essence of Islamic faith according to the Qur'an, is centered on the concept of monotheism - verily, it is the core of the religion. The vast majority of the message of Islam, and the Qur'an focuses on monotheism. The Lord asserts in the Qur'an that no Prophet was sent to mankind, but to invite people to worship God.

وَمَآ أَرۡسَلۡنَا مِن قَبۡلِكَ مِن رَّسُولٍ إِلَّا نُوحِيٓ إِلَيۡهِ أَنَّهُۥ لَآ إِلَٰهَ إِلَّآ أَنَا۠ فَٱعۡبُدُونِ

> And We sent no messenger before you except that We revealed to him: "Verily, there is no god except Me; so worship Me!"[1]

The Qur'an stresses that every single Prophet came with this prime message to invite people to believe in and serve God, since God is the 'Essential Existence' in this universe (*Wajib al-Wujud*).

Muslims believe that they are only accountable to God. Therefore, it is imperative that all Muslims have a clear and concise understanding of the concept of monotheism. God's act of sending messengers, starting with Adam, was solely done in order to convey this concept to mankind. Therefore, it is paramount that monotheism is at the heart of all of the actions performed by Muslims on a daily basis.

There is a vigorous discussion amongst the various schools of thought within Islam centered on the concept of monotheism.

---

[1] Qur'an, Surah al-Anbiya (21), verse 25.

While certain acts are considered to be part of monotheism for some, the same acts may be considered heresy to others. It is incumbent upon Muslims to examine which traditions, customs, and types of worshipping comply with the spirit of monotheism in the Qur'an.

One of the strongest proponents of monotheism in ancient times was Prophet Abraham, the patriarch, who vehemently advocated, promoted, and delivered the message of monotheism to his community in Babylonia. This community consisted of idol worshippers. When Prophet Abraham invited them to worship God, his requests were denied and he was ultimately persecuted and thrown into a raging fire. As a result of that, God ordered him to leave Babylonia and travel to Palestine. As per God's order, Prophet Abraham went to Palestine and invited the people there to monotheism. He married Sarah, and then also married Hagar, who bore him a son named Ishmael. After the birth of Ishmael, God ordered Prophet Abraham to take both Hagar and Ishmael to Mecca. Before Sarah bore him their son Isaac, Prophet Abraham acted on God's commands and left with Hagar and Ishmael for Mecca.

رَّبَّنَآ إِنِّيٓ أَسۡكَنتُ مِن ذُرِّيَّتِي بِوَادٍ غَيۡرِ ذِي زَرۡعٍ عِندَ بَيۡتِكَ ٱلۡمُحَرَّمِ

> Our Lord! Verily I have settled some of my progeny in a valley without cultivation near Your Sacred House.[2]

The Archangel Gabriel showed Prophet Abraham the original site of the House of God (the Ka'bah). The Ka'bah had been built by Prophet Adam, only to be destroyed at a later stage by the great flood during the time of Prophet Noah. Prophet Abraham

---

[2] Qur'an, Surah Ibrahim (14), verse 37.

and his son, Ishmael, rebuilt the Ka'bah at this same site in Mecca.

وَإِذْ يَرْفَعُ إِبْرَٰهِـۧمُ ٱلْقَوَاعِدَ مِنَ ٱلْبَيْتِ وَإِسْمَٰعِيلُ رَبَّنَا تَقَبَّلْ مِنَّآ ۖ إِنَّكَ أَنتَ ٱلسَّمِيعُ ٱلْعَلِيمُ

> And [remember] when Abraham and Ishmael were raising the foundations of the House (they said): "Our Lord, accept [it] from us. Surely You are the Hearing, the Knowing.[3]

Prophet Abraham's work as a builder was performed with the utmost sincerity and dedication to God. When the building of the Ka'bah was completed, Prophet Abraham invited people to come to Mecca in order to perform pilgrimage. As the Qur'an mentions, contextually, Mecca was a valley without cultivation, nor inhabitants. However, after the discovery of the well of Zamzam (following Hagar's frantic search for water for her son Ishmael who was dying of thirst), the popularity of Mecca grew. An Arab tribe by the name of Jurhum passed by and noticed birds in the area which was an indication that there must have been water there. This tribe became the first to permanently settle in Mecca.

Prophet Abraham and his son Ishmael were the first people to perform the pilgrimage and circumambulate around the House of God with the help of Archangel Gabriel. After Prophet Abraham's death in Hebron, Palestine, Prophet Ishmael continued his father's work of inviting people to monotheism until he passed away. Ishmael's death in Mecca meant that he was consequently buried right beside the House of God.

The passing of years brought about a shift in people's mentalities and beliefs; and the people of Mecca diverted from

---

[3] Qur'an, Surah al-Baqarah (2), verse 127.

the course of monotheism. Idol worshipping was introduced to the Arabian Peninsula by a man from Mecca by the name of Amr ibn Lahi. He was a merchant who used to travel to Syria for business. Syria, which was a part of the Roman Empire at the time, contained a vast number of idol worshippers, something that Amr noticed on his business trips to the region. Amr ibn Lahi went to the pagans and asked them what they were worshipping. They replied that they worshipped deities from whom they asked for all of their needs, such as rain, health, and sustenance; and that the deities in turn, responded to them. Amr liked the idea, and decided to purchase an idol by the name of Hubal and transfer it to Mecca. He invited the Meccans to worship the idol with the promise that it would answer all of their prayers. He told the Meccans to pray to this idol if they needed any assistance. Being able to have a physical, visible, and tangible deity right before their eyes attracted the people of Mecca to worship the idol.

Historians and philosophers alike believe that there were many reasons why people shifted from worshipping God to worshipping idols. The main explanation that is given is that of a psychological need - people tend to believe in things that they can see before their eyes, just like the pagans in Arabia did when they were able to see Hubal, their new "deity." It is much easier for people to believe in things that are tangible, visible, or accessible. When average individuals experience the physical presence of an object, they will be more inclined to believe in it and embrace it. Whereas if the object is invisible, or not easily accessible, then it will be harder for people to accept it. Therefore, it is difficult for some people to believe in God when they are told that they cannot see, approach, or fully comprehend Him.

The Difference between the Physical and Spiritual Approach of Seeing God

Central to the drive in the belief in the Divinity of Jesus within the Christian faith is having visual access to statues, paintings, and other depictions of him. This ocular representation of Jesus was the work of Saint Paul, who aspired to make Christianity more accessible to the masses, as well as to attract the pagans.

Churches, especially the Catholic ones, are decorated with statues, portraits, and illustrations of the divinities in the form of Jesus and Mary. A major part of the Catholic tradition is based on art depicting Jesus, his disciples, and those who are important within the Christian traditions. These visualisations often help in bringing the image of God closer to the minds of the believers; and it gives the idea that God is neither absent, nor far away. The Islamic approach, however, differs from its Christian counterpart, as it is based on a spiritual and mental approach.

وَلَقَدْ خَلَقْنَا ٱلْإِنسَٰنَ وَنَعْلَمُ مَا تُوَسْوِسُ بِهِۦ نَفْسُهُۥ ۖ وَنَحْنُ أَقْرَبُ إِلَيْهِ مِنْ حَبْلِ ٱلْوَرِيدِ

> We indeed created man, and We know what his soul whispers to him; and We are nearer to him than his jugular vein.[4]

Through the mental and spiritual growth of a human mind, one is able to realize that the vast majority of spiritual entities in this universe are invisible. What we are able to see and touch in this universe is a fraction of what God has created. Therefore, the lack of ability to physically see something, does not negate its existence. When we do not see God with our eyes, it does not mean that He is absent - it only means that our vision is limited.

---

[4] Qur'an, Surah Qaaf (50), verse 16.

However, God has given us great inner vision, allowing us to see His signs that lead to Him. In brief, God is Transcendent, yet Imminent.

The reverent ones are able to feel the presence of God in their hearts. In the beginning of the Qur'an, God explains that the first sign of reverence is the belief in the Unseen:

هُدًى لِّلْمُتَّقِينَ ۝ ٱلَّذِينَ يُؤْمِنُونَ بِٱلْغَيْبِ

> A guidance for the reverent, who believe in the Unseen.[5]

Imam Ali provided an eloquent interpretation when he was asked by one of his companions, Thalab al-Yamani, whether he had seen his Lord. The Imam replied: "How can I worship something that I do not see?" When asked how he saw Him, Imam Ali replied:

لاَ تُدْرِكُهُ الْعُيُونُ بِمُشَاهَدَةِ الْعِيَانِ، وَلكِنْ تُدْرِكُهُ الْقُلُوبُ بِحَقَائِقِ الأْيمَانِ

> "Eyes do not reach Him with the physical sight, but hearts reach Him with the realities of belief."[6]

We do not and cannot witness God with our eyes; nevertheless, our heart and conscience testify the existence of Him. In fact, the inner vision and the ability to use reason to explain His existence are far more profound and compelling than that of the physical senses; thus, God does not need to present Himself to His creatures through an image or a statue.

The most practical and effective method of communicating with God is done by concentration of the heart and enunciation of the tongue, as God states in the Qur'an:

---

[5] Qur'an, Surah al-Baqarah (2), verses 2-3.

[6] *Nahj al-Balagha*, Sermon 179.

يَٰٓأَيُّهَا ٱلَّذِينَ ءَامَنُواْ ٱذۡكُرُواْ ٱللَّهَ ذِكۡرٗا كَثِيرٗا ۝ وَسَبِّحُوهُ بُكۡرَةٗ
وَأَصِيلًا

> O you who believe! Remember God with frequent remembrance, and glorify Him morning and evening.[7]

This remembrance requires meditation and reflection. A special time should be dedicated to this process where the mind is focused, and the heart is connected. In order to reap the benefits, one should strive to make this process frequent and do it continuously.

[7] Qur'an, Surah al-Ahzaab (33), verses 41-42.

2

Meaning of Monotheism

إِنَّنِيٓ أَنَا ٱللَّهُ لَآ إِلَٰهَ إِلَّآ أَنَا۠ فَٱعْبُدْنِي

> Truly, I am God, there is no deity except Me, so worship Me (alone).[1]

[1] Qur'an, Surah Taha (20), verse 14.

In the previous chapter, we established that the concept of monotheism forms the quintessence of the Islamic faith. Furthermore, we established that God does not need to have physical manifestations through images and statues, but rather through inner vision and consciousness, we can begin to make a deeper and more conscious connection with Him.

The story of an atheist teacher and his students illustrate this concept very well. A first grade teacher was once promoting his belief that God does not exist. While pointing out various objects in his classroom, the teacher asked his students whether they could see these objects or not? The students responded in the affirmative. Then, the teacher followed up by asking if they could see God. Since his students agreed that they could not see God, he concluded that the objects which he pointed out exist, but God does not exist. An intelligent student in the class requested to say something. He inquired whether his classmates could see the teacher's brain. Obviously, the students could not see it, so the student concluded that the teacher does not have a brain. The teacher was dumbfounded by this response. In doing so, this student sent a powerful message that just because we cannot see a certain thing, it does not mean that it is nonexistent.

In addition to the belief in God's amorphous nature, the concept of God's Unity entails the belief that only God should be worshipped, for He does not have any associates or partners. God is the only Self-Sufficient being in this entire universe, meaning that He is totally free from all needs - be it material or spiritual.

Prophet Muhammad extended an invitation to the People of the Book in Medina for a common word: to worship God and only God, and to withdraw from any associates or partners with Him.

قُلْ يَٰٓأَهْلَ ٱلْكِتَٰبِ تَعَالَوْا۟ إِلَىٰ كَلِمَةٍ سَوَآءٍۭ بَيْنَنَا وَبَيْنَكُمْ أَلَّا نَعْبُدَ إِلَّا ٱللَّهَ

> Say: "O People of the Book! Come to a word common between us and you - that we shall worship none except God."[1]

The Qur'an states that the negation of the existence of God, or taking associates or partners with Him, is an insult to one's intelligence and intellectual integrity.

إِنَّ ٱللَّهَ لَا يَغْفِرُ أَن يُشْرَكَ بِهِۦ

> Verily God will not forgive that any partner be ascribed unto Him.[2]

Muslim scholars differentiate between the words *kufr* (atheism) and *shirk* (polytheism). Each one has a specific meaning in the Qur'an as follows:

- *Kufr*: Denying the existence of God, and in some cases, taking partners with God.
- *Shirk*: Believing in the existence of God, while also worshipping other objects alongside God.

وَلَئِن سَأَلْتَهُم مَّنْ خَلَقَ ٱلسَّمَٰوَٰتِ وَٱلْأَرْضَ لَيَقُولُنَّ ٱللَّهُ

> And if you were to ask them: "Who created the heavens and the earth?" they would surely say: "God."[3]

The above verse provides a clear example of an act of *shirk* (polytheism, apostasy, and heresy). Although the pagans referenced in this verse believed that God created the heavens

---

[1] Qur'an, Surah Ale Imraan (3), verse 64.
[2] Qur'an, Surah al-Nisaa (4), verse 48.
[3] Qur'an, Surah Luqmaan (31), verse 25.

and earth, nonetheless they also believed that God was associated with other powerful entities. This means that they believed in His existence, but did not believe in His Omnipotence.

The Real Meaning of "*Allahu Akbar*"

قال: قال رجل عنده: الله أكبر. فقال: الله أكبر من أي شيء؟ فقال: من كلّ شيء. فقال أبو عبد الله (عليه السلام): حددته! فقال الرجل: كيف أقول؟ قال: قل: الله أكبر مِن أن يوصف

> A companion of Imam al-Sadiq said: "Once (Imam) Abu 'Abd Allah asked me: 'What is the meaning of Allahu Akbar?' I replied: 'Allah is the greatest of all things.' The Imam further asked: 'Were there other things so Allah could be considered the greatest of them?' I then questioned: 'What then is the meaning thereof?' The Imam replied: 'Allah is by far greater. He is beyond all descriptions.'"[4]

God is unlimited; He is beyond space and time, thus He is too great to be understood by man. With an average of 15 billion cells, our brains - no matter how perfect - are still incapable of understanding the reality of God. What we know about God is very limited, yet even this limited knowledge about Him amazes us.

Thus, this begs the question: How can something that is limited understand an unlimited God? It requires more than intelligence to grasp the full understanding of God! It requires God's Grace and Revelation. It has been said that God presented

---

[4] *Usul al-Kafi*, vol. 1, pg. 117.

His full recognition to Prophet Muhammad, and he in turn passed that special knowledge on to his disciple, Imam Ali.

يا علي، ما عرف الله إلا أنا وأنت

> O Ali, only me and you are able to truly understand God.[5]

In one of his sermons, the best student of the Prophet of Islam, Imam Ali ibn Abi Talib, describes the meaning and details of monotheism in a way that no other person can ever explain. Among what he said is:

مَا وَحَّدَهُ مَنْ كَيَّفَهُ، وَلاَ حَقِيقَتَهُ أَصَابَ مَنْ مَثَّلَهُ، وَلاَ إِيَّاهُ عَنَى مَنْ شَبَّهَهُ، وَلاَ صَمَدَهُ مَنْ أَشَارَ إِلَيْهِ وَتَوَهَّمَهُ. كُلُّ مَعْرُوف بِنَفْسِهِ مَصْنُوعٌ، وَكُلُّ قَائِم فِي سِوَاهُ مَعْلُولٌ. فَاعِلٌ لاَ بِاضْطِرَابِ آلَة، مُقَدِّرٌ لاَ بِجَوْلِ فِكْرَة، غَنِيٌّ لاَ بِاسْتِفَادَة.

> The person who assigns to Him (different) conditions does not believe in His Oneness, nor does one who likens Him grasp His reality. The one who illustrates Him does not signify Him. The one who points at Him and imagines Him does not mean Him. Everything that is known through itself has been created, and everything that exists by virtue of other things is the effect (of a cause). He works but not with the help of instruments. He fixes measures but not with the activity of thinking. He is rich but not by acquisition.[6]

---

[5] *Al-Manaaqib*, Ibn Shahr Ashub, vol. 3, pg. 267; *Irshaad Al-Quloob*, Al-Daylami, pg. 209.

[6] *Nahj al-Balagha*, Sermon 186.

Branches of Monotheism

Monotheism and worshipping God have been meticulously defined in the Qur'an, and are explained in the following chapters, by way of the five main branches of monotheism (*Furu' al-Tawheed*):

1. The Unity of God's Essence (*Tawheed al-Dhaat*)
2. The Unity of God's Attributes (*Tawheed al-Sifaat)*
3. The Unity of God's Deeds (*Tahweed al-Af'aal)*
4. The Unity of Worshipping God (*Tawheed al-Ibaadah*)
5. The Unity and Integrity of God's Guardianship (*Tawheed al-Walaayah*)

3

Unity of God's Essence (*Tawheed al-Dhaat*)

قُلْ هُوَ ٱللَّهُ أَحَدٌ ۝ ٱللَّهُ ٱلصَّمَدُ ۝ لَمْ يَلِدْ وَلَمْ يُولَدْ ۝ وَلَمْ
يَكُن لَّهُۥ كُفُوًا أَحَدٌۢ

> Say: "He, God, is One, God, the Eternally Sufficient unto Himself. He begets not; nor was He begotten. And none is like unto Him."[1]

[1] Qur'an, Surah al-Ikhlaas (112), verses 1-4.

The first dimension of monotheism is the Unity of the Essence of God (*Tawheed al-Dhaat*). To understand the Essence of God, one has to review what the essence of a human being is. People are composed of a visible physical part - the body, and an invisible spiritual part - the soul (*ruh*). The Qur'an alludes to this fact in the following verse:

فَإِذَا سَوَّيْتُهُۥ وَنَفَخْتُ فِيهِ مِن رُّوحِى

> "So when I have proportioned him and breathed into him of My soul."[1]

Unlike human beings, God is not composed of a physical and spiritual part. Instead, the Essence of God can be explained with the concepts of *Al-Waahadiyyah* and *Al-Ahadiyyah*.

Al-Waahadiyyah means that God is Unique. There is nothing in this universe that resembles or matches God. While the general meaning of '*waahid*' in Arabic is 'one,' *waahid* does not refer to a number when discussing God's Essence. It means that there is none like God, hence there is no image or likeness of Him; a concept which is foundational in the Qur'an.

وَلَمْ يَكُن لَّهُۥ كُفُوًا أَحَدُۢ

> And none is like unto Him.[2]

لَيْسَ كَمِثْلِهِۦ شَىْءٌ

> There is nothing like unto Him.[3]

Scholars argue that it is wrong to say that God is one with the vision of one being a numerical adjective. The Divine Unity is

---

[1] Qur'an, Surah al-Hijr (15), verse 29.
[2] Qur'an, Surah al-Ikhlaas (112), verse 4.
[3] Qur'an, Surah al-Shura (42), verse 11.

ontological (beyond numerical). In *Nahj al-Balagha*, Imam Ali describes God by saying:

وَلاَ يُحْسَبُ بِعَدٍّ

> Nor (is He) counted by numbers.[4]

God is not counted by numbers, because number one is followed by number two, number two is followed by number three, and so on. Numbers stand for multiplicity. Therefore, one cannot use one as a number for God, since He is Unmatched and Unique.

Imagine that there is an entity which fills a certain space, leaving no extra space for another entity to join. Similarly, God fills the entire space, but even then He is not limited by time, nor is He constrained by space, leaving no room for a second deity to exist. Therefore, God enjoys numerical integrity (*Al-Wahdah al-'Adadiyyah).*

In the battle of the Camel, Imam Ali explained the Oneness of God to a man as follows:

فقول القائل: واحد يقصد به باب الأعداد، فهذا ما لا يجوز، لأن ما لا ثاني له لا يدخل في باب الأعداد

> If someone says "one" regarding God, and intended this numerically, then this is not permissible because He who does not have a second, cannot be counted numerically.[5]

Imam Ali further stated:

> A person who describes Him, limits Him; one who limits Him, numbers Him; and one who numbers Him, denies His pre-eternity.[6]

---

[4] *Nahj al-Balagha*, Sermon 186.
[5] *Book of Tawheed,* Al-Sadooq, pg. 83.
[6] *Nahj al-Balagha*, Sermon 152.

Sermon 65 of *Nahj al-Balagha* describes the notion of God being the First and the Last. Being the First does not contradict Him being the Last, since notions of "first" and "last" are temporal limitations that apply to creatures, but not to God.

The different Attributes of God do not entail His multiplicity. For instance, the Qur'an uses the terms *Elah* and *Allah* to refer to God:

إِنَّنِيٓ أَنَا ٱللَّهُ لَآ إِلَٰهَ إِلَّآ أَنَا۠

> Truly I am God, there is no deity except Me.[7]

While the expression is different, the essence is the same. *Elah* is the deity, and Allah is God. The general expression is *Elah*, while the specific name is Allah.

Besides the terms *Elah* and *Allah*, there are ninety-nine other names which refer to the Attributes of God. They all refer to Him as One Entity and One Essence. These names represent His Characters and Attributes, not multiple entities. God may express Himself through different Attributes, as will be explained in the next chapter.

The second concept of the Unity of God's Essence is *Al-'Ahadiyyah.* It means that the Essence of God is unstructured, unassembled, and simple without any complexity (*Dhatuhu Basita).* God is not made up of various parts that are assembled together, as it has been conceived by followers of other religions. If God had been structured and composed of several parts, then in order for Him to function, each part of Him would be in need of the other parts to work in unison. This would make God in need, violating the concept of God's Self-Sufficiency. Islam asserts that God is free from all forms of needs, including the

---

[7] Qur'an, Surah Taha (20), verse 14.

need of Himself as well. The concept of *Al-'Ahadiyyah* is mentioned in several verses of the Qur'an, for example:

قُلْ هُوَ ٱللَّهُ أَحَدٌ

> Say, "He, God, is One."[8]

وَقَالَ ٱللَّهُ لَا تَتَّخِذُوٓا۟ إِلَـٰهَيْنِ ٱثْنَيْنِ ۖ إِنَّمَا هُوَ إِلَـٰهٌ وَٰحِدٌ

> And God says: "Do not take up (for yourselves) two deities. Truly He is only one God."[9]

At the time of the birth of Islam, the Jews in Arabia believed in two idols named *Jibt* and *Taghut*, each of whom had their own given tasks. *Jibt* was the idol associated with sorcery, and *Taghut* was the idol associated with evil-doing.

أَلَمْ تَرَ إِلَى ٱلَّذِينَ أُوتُوا۟ نَصِيبًا مِّنَ ٱلْكِتَـٰبِ يُؤْمِنُونَ بِٱلْجِبْتِ وَٱلطَّـٰغُوتِ وَيَقُولُونَ لِلَّذِينَ كَفَرُوا۟ هَـٰٓؤُلَآءِ أَهْدَىٰ مِنَ ٱلَّذِينَ ءَامَنُوا۟ سَبِيلًا

> Have you not seen those who were given a portion of the Book, who believe in *Jibt* and *Taghut*, and say about the disbelievers: "These are guided more rightly than those who believe (as to the) way."[10]

The pagan Arabs believed in these same idols, *Jibt* and *Taghut*, until the arrival of Islam, when the Qur'an asserted:

إِنَّمَا هُوَ إِلَـٰهٌ وَٰحِدٌ

> Truly He is only one God.[11]

---

[8] Qur'an, Surah al-Ikhlaas (112), verse 1.
[9] Qur'an, Surah al-Nahl (16), verse 51.
[10] Qur'an, Surah al-Nisaa (4), verse 51.
[11] Qur'an, Surah al-Nahl (16), verse 51.

The deities of the pagans were endowed with different tasks, such as bestowing rain upon the earth, cultivating agriculture, providing sustenance, bestowing health and children, etc. For them, it was as if these deities were working together to respond to their worshippers. The pagans were shocked to hear the Prophet preach that there is only one God who provides for everyone without the help of another being. The concept of God's Uniqueness was incomprehensible to their simple minds. The Qur'an mentions the pagans' reaction to the Prophet as follows:

أَجَعَلَ ٱلْآلِهَةَ إِلَٰهًا وَٰحِدًا ۖ إِنَّ هَٰذَا لَشَىْءٌ عُجَابٌ

> Has he made the gods (only) one God? Truly this is an astounding thing!"[12]

The remnants of paganism endured even after the advent of Islam. When God ordained the Muslims to perform Hajj, the new Arab converts to Islam were hesitant to march between the mountains of Safa and Marwa because idols were previously placed on them. Before the arrival of Islam in Mecca, the Arabs had brought two idols, supposedly male and female, which they erected on Mounts Safa and Marwa. They marched between them and bowed before them.

To address the Muslim's hesitation, the Qur'an says:

إِنَّ ٱلصَّفَا وَٱلْمَرْوَةَ مِن شَعَآئِرِ ٱللَّهِ ۖ فَمَنْ حَجَّ ٱلْبَيْتَ أَوِ ٱعْتَمَرَ فَلَا جُنَاحَ عَلَيْهِ أَن يَطَّوَّفَ بِهِمَا ۚ وَمَن تَطَوَّعَ خَيْرًا فَإِنَّ ٱللَّهَ شَاكِرٌ عَلِيمٌ

[12] Qur'an, Surah Saad (38), verse 5.

> Truly Safa and Marwa are among the rites of God; so whosoever performs the Hajj to the House, or makes the Umrah, there is no blame on them in marching between them. And whosoever volunteers good, then surely God is All-Thankful, All-Knowing.[13]

The Qur'an asserts that although these mountains are made of rocks, they are among the signs or symbols of God - regardless of whether they were once defiled by idols or not.

Monotheism opposes the concept of dualism, or the coexistence of deities as it compromises the integrity of God. Contrary to the concept of dualism, the Qur'an speaks about the concepts of God's Uniqueness and the Integrity of His Essence. For example, chapter 112 states that God does not have any rival nor a match; He is Unique and Unparalleled. It is also apparent that the last verse of this same chapter refers to the concept of God's Uniqueness (*Al-Waahadiyyah*), whereas the first verse refers to the concept of the Unity of His Essence (*Al-Ahadiyyah).*

---

[13] Qur'an, Surah al-Baqarah (2), verse 158.

4

Unity of God’s Attributes (*Tawheed al-Sifaat*)

هُوَ ٱللَّهُ ٱلَّذِى لَآ إِلَـٰهَ إِلَّا هُوَ ٱلْمَلِكُ ٱلْقُدُّوسُ ٱلسَّلَـٰمُ ٱلْمُؤْمِنُ
ٱلْمُهَيْمِنُ ٱلْعَزِيزُ ٱلْجَبَّارُ ٱلْمُتَكَبِّرُ ۚ سُبْحَـٰنَ ٱللَّهِ عَمَّا يُشْرِكُونَ هُوَ
ٱللَّهُ ٱلْخَـٰلِقُ ٱلْبَارِئُ ٱلْمُصَوِّرُ ۖ لَهُ ٱلْأَسْمَآءُ ٱلْحُسْنَىٰ ۚ يُسَبِّحُ لَهُۥ مَا
فِى ٱلسَّمَـٰوَٰتِ وَٱلْأَرْضِ ۖ وَهُوَ ٱلْعَزِيزُ ٱلْحَكِيمُ

> He is God, other than Whom there is no deity, the Sovereign, the Holy, the (Giver of) Peace, the Faithful, the Protector, the Mighty, the Compeller, the Proud. Glory be to Him above the partners they ascribe (with Him). He is God, the Creator, the Maker, the Fashioner; to Him belong the Most Beautiful Names. Whatsoever is in the heavens and the earth glorifies Him; and He is the All-Mighty, the All-Wise.[1]

[1] Qur’an, Surah al-Hashr (59), verses 23-24.

The second dimension of monotheism is the Unity of God's Attributes or Characteristics (*Tawheed al-Sifaat).* God's Attributes are exactly His Essence, because His Attributes and His Essence are inseparable. God is Omniscient, Omnipotent, Infinite, and Omnipresent which means that His possession of these qualities is in perpetuum. He permanently and eternally possesses these Attributes. His Knowledge, Power, Limitlessness, and Presence are not in addition to His Essence. In fact, they are the core of His Essence.

In the third century of the Islamic Calendar (Hijri), a group of Islamic philosophers known as *Al-Karamiyyah*, believed that the Characteristics of God were created after His Essence. Other Islamic schools of thought refuted this claim, asserting that the Essence of God is His Character, and His Character is His Essence.

الصفات عين الذات والذات عين الصفات

> God's Attributes are His Essence, and His Essence are His Attributes.

God is the only self-subsisting entity and the only Sovereign Power in this entire universe. All abilities rely on God, but God's Abilities are reliant on none. His existence is Absolute, while everything else's existence is conditional upon Him. He is the Creator of everything, but nothing created Him.

The Verse of the Throne

The "Verse of the Throne" called "*Ayat al-Kursi*" from the second chapter "The Cow" speaks about monotheism and the Attributes and Wonders of God. This verse has been depicted as the "Jewel of the Qur'an." It consists of fifty words, and every word is a blessing. Prophet Muhammad advised Imam Ali to recite the "Verse of the Throne" as a means to seek refuge from every malice. A narration mentions that if a person recites "*Ayat al-Kursi*" once, then God will assign an angel to safeguard him. If someone recites it twice, then God will assign two angels for safeguarding. If an individual recites it thrice, then God Himself will watch over them. This verse 255 of Surah al-Baqarah is as follows:

ٱللَّهُ لَآ إِلَٰهَ إِلَّا هُوَ ٱلْحَىُّ ٱلْقَيُّومُ

> God, there is no deity except Him, the Ever-Living, the Self-Subsisting.

The verse describes that God is the only entity in this universe that is Self-Sustained, while the entire universe depends on God for its sustenance.

لَا تَأْخُذُهُۥ سِنَةٌ وَلَا نَوْمٌ

> Neither slumber overtakes Him nor sleep.

While man needs to sleep and rest to be able to function properly, God is always awake and attentive.

لَّهُۥ مَا فِى ٱلسَّمَٰوَٰتِ وَمَا فِى ٱلْأَرْضِ

> To Him belongs whatsoever is in the heavens and whatsoever is on the earth.

He is the Lord of everything in existence, from the heavens to the earth, and all things belong to Him alone.

مَن ذَا ٱلَّذِى يَشْفَعُ عِندَهُۥٓ إِلَّا بِإِذْنِهِ

> Who is there who may intercede with Him except by His permission?

The right of intercession only belongs to Him, and absolutely no one else can intercede unless He allows it.

يَعْلَمُ مَا بَيْنَ أَيْدِيهِمْ وَمَا خَلْفَهُمْ

> He knows that which is before them and that which is behind them.

When it comes to the future, man's knowledge is very limited. Man can spend time making the best plans, yet only God knows what will actually transpire, for He is Omniscient.

وَلَا يُحِيطُونَ بِشَيْءٍ مِّنْ عِلْمِهِۦٓ إِلَّا بِمَا شَآءَ

> And they encompass nothing of His Knowledge, except what He wills.

Only God has knowledge of the Unseen and decides who He shares His Knowledge with.

وَسِعَ كُرْسِيُّهُ ٱلسَّمَٰوَٰتِ وَٱلْأَرْضَ

> His Throne embraces the heavens and the earth.

Some interpreters refer to the "*Kursi*" as the Pedestal that encompasses the heavens and the earth, and the Throne (*Arsh*) as encompassing the Pedestal. It is a metaphor of God's Sovereignty and Authority.

وَلَا يَـُٔودُهُۥ حِفْظُهُمَا ۚ وَهُوَ ٱلْعَلِىُّ ٱلْعَظِيمُ

> Protecting them tires Him not, and He is the Exalted, the Magnificent.

While humans can get exhausted by performing their duties, because of their limited capabilities, God's role as the Creator and the Controller never exhausts Him. He is All-Powerful and Omnipotent, and His Power encompasses everything in the entire universe.

The Difference between God's Attributes and Man's Attributes

وَهُوَ ٱلۡقَاهِرُ فَوۡقَ عِبَادِهِۦ

> And He is Dominant over His servants.[1]

The inability to comprehend one's surroundings is a feature that every human being is born with when they come into this world. Slowly, and with the passing of time, a person will start to grasp one's surroundings and acquire the knowledge which will aid in one's development and survival within this world. Everything that human beings possess or know, was not innately within them when they were born, thus all that they have acquired from birth, could very well be lost as they age. On the other hand, God's Knowledge has always been innately within Him and does not ever fluctuate. He is All-Knowing, and His Knowledge is Eternal, and He oversees the creation of all objects in this universe.

When it comes to God's Beneficence and people's generosity, there is a clear distinction as well - human beings are not generous from the first day of their existence. In stark contrast, God was and always is All-Generous. His Generosity and Kindness are a part of His Essence which are inseparable and indivisible. Every Attribute of God is embedded within His Essence.

The lack of power is another feature of every human being. The difference between God's Power and man's power can be understood in three brief points:

1. **God is Self-Powered.** His Power is Self-Generated and has always existed since the beginning of time; it neither

---

[1] Qur'an, Surah al-An'aam (6), verse 18.

fluctuates, nor comes from an external source. Man's power on the other hand, is from God and dependent solely upon God. Therefore, one must constantly seek help and power from God. The following is a phrase of remembrance (*dhikr*) that has been attributed to the Prophet who used to recite it on a regular basis:

لَا حَوْلَ وَلَا قُوَّةَ إِلَّا بِٱللَّهِ ٱلْعَلِيِّ ٱلْعَظِيمِ

> "There is no power, nor strength except in God, the Lofty, the Great."

Man can become arrogant once he possesses some power, forgetting that ultimately all power only belongs to Almighty God. The Qur'an quotes Pharaoh, who used to tell his subjugates the following:

فَقَالَ أَنَا رَبُّكُمُ الْأَعْلَى

> Then he said: "I am your lord, the most high."[2]

Only when Pharaoh was drowning in the sea did he accept that the Lord who Moses had told him about was in fact the true Lord. However, it was too late for him to assert his belief, when he knew that his death had approached.

2. **God is Self-Sufficient.** He does not need anyone or anything, but everyone and everything else needs Him.

يَٰٓأَيُّهَا ٱلنَّاسُ أَنتُمُ ٱلْفُقَرَآءُ إِلَى ٱللَّهِ ۖ وَٱللَّهُ هُوَ ٱلْغَنِيُّ ٱلْحَمِيدُ

> O mankind! You are needful of God; and He is the Self-Sufficient, the Praised.[3]

---

[2] Qur'an, Surah al-Naaziat (79), verse 24.
[3] Qur'an, Surah Faatir (35), verse 15.

According to Imam Ali, the more powerful a person becomes, the more one needs God.

3. **God is the only Sovereign** and the absolute Independent Power in the entire universe. He does not depend on anyone or anything, while everyone and everything else depends on Him.

قُلْ مَنۢ بِيَدِهِۦ مَلَكُوتُ كُلِّ شَىْءٍ وَهُوَ يُجِيرُ وَلَا يُجَارُ عَلَيْهِ إِن كُنتُمْ تَعْلَمُونَ

> Say: "Who is it in Whose Hand lies the dominion of everything, who protects but is not protected against, if you know?"[4]

The Most Important Attributes of God

Omniscience

It is not correct to state that there was a point in time when God's Knowledge was limited about a certain issue, and then He became knowledgeable about that. God's Knowledge has always been a part of Him and it does not fluctuate. He knew about us before we even came into existence. Our parents, who were the vessels for our arrival into this world and were instrumental in our conception, only came to know about us when we were conceived, but not before that. However, God knew about the details of our characteristics, our souls, deeds, achievements, failures, successes, and all of our secrets, before we even entered into this world.

---

[4] Qur'an, Surah al-Mominoon (23), verse 88.

وَعِندَهُۥ مَفَاتِحُ ٱلْغَيْبِ لَا يَعْلَمُهَآ إِلَّا هُوَ ۚ وَيَعْلَمُ مَا فِى ٱلْبَرِّ
وَٱلْبَحْرِ ۚ وَمَا تَسْقُطُ مِن وَرَقَةٍ إِلَّا يَعْلَمُهَا وَلَا حَبَّةٍ فِى ظُلُمَٰتِ
ٱلْأَرْضِ وَلَا رَطْبٍ وَلَا يَابِسٍ إِلَّا فِى كِتَٰبٍ مُّبِينٍ

> And with Him are the keys of the Unseen. None knows them but He; and He knows what is on the land and in the sea; no leaf falls but He knows it, nor any seed in the dark recesses of the earth, nor anything moist or dry, but that it is (all) in a clear Book.[5]

Omnipotence

God is All-Powerful and Omnipotent. His Power and Authority were not bestowed upon Him at any time, as He has always been Powerful and Sovereign. He is Eternal and His Power never diminishes, nor fluctuates.

Unlike monarchs and leaders (who are powerful one day, but powerless the next), God is eternally Able and Powerful.

God describes Himself as Able (*Qaadir*):

إِنَّا لَقَٰدِرُونَ

> Indeed We are Able.[6]

He also describes Himself as Irresistible (*Qahaar*):

وَهُوَ ٱلْوَٰحِدُ ٱلْقَهَّٰرُ

> And He is the One, the Irresistible.[7]

---

[5] Qur'an, Surah al-An'aam (6), verse 59.
[6] Qur'an, Surah al-Ma'arij (70), verse 40.
[7] Qur'an, Surah al-Ra'd (13), verse 16.

لا تقهره القيود ولا يسلب منه شيء

> No conditions defy God, and He cannot be stripped of anything.

It is irrefutable that humans may one day be irresistible and conquering (*Qaahir*), while another day their power may diminish, which will then result in being conquered and defeated (*Maqhur*). Take the example of a dictator from the Middle East. The citizens of his country, including his most trusted ministers feared looking at him, let alone have the courage to talk to him. It was the norm that people would bow their heads when they conversed with him, and they would be expected to address him as "my master." His own family members could not look him in the eyes due to his savagery and brutality. That same dictator was captured from a hole, where he had been hiding without any helper or defender. In his final days, he was defenseless and humiliated, and had no recourse to any loyalty which was outwardly displayed to him during his tyrannical reign. Unlike such dictators, God is eternally Powerful and the Ultimate Conqueror. Nothing can resist His Power and Will.

وَهُوَ ٱلْقَاهِرُ فَوْقَ عِبَادِهِ

> And He is Dominant over His servants.[8]

Omnipresence

Another attribute of God is His Omnipresence. God has a strong and absolute presence everywhere.

---

[8] Qur'an, Surah al-An'aam (6), verse 18.

وَهُوَ مَعَكُمْ أَيْنَ مَا كُنتُمْ

> And He is with you wherever you are.[9]

فَأَيْنَمَا تُوَلُّوا۟ فَثَمَّ وَجْهُ ٱللَّهِ

> So wherever you turn, there is the Face of God.[10]

No matter where a person goes, God is present there without any limitations or restrictions. According to Islamic beliefs, Prophet Jesus is seen as being fully human, not as divine. As with every human being, Jesus' mortality means that he is limited. If he were to be present in one place, then he cannot simultaneously be present in another place. Even though his message can reach far and wide, he himself is still confined within space and time, whereas God is neither confined nor restricted by anything at all.

A question may arise for some people that if God is Omnipresent, then why is it that Muslims are obliged to visit Mecca for the pilgrimage? Why not call upon God in one's own home?

Muslims travel this great distance not only to find God in Mecca, but also because God has invited believers to visit His House in Mecca during the pilgrimage season to gather in a universal convention, to experience a special spiritual feeling, to solidify their unity, and to enjoy numerous other benefits.

لِّيَشْهَدُوا مَنَافِعَ لَهُمْ

> That they may witness benefits for themselves.[11]

Going on pilgrimage to Mecca, circumambulating around His House, and performing other rites, enhances our understanding

---

[9] Qur'an, Surah al-Hadeed (57), verse 4.
[10] Qur'an, Surah al-Baqarah (2), verse 115.
[11] Qur'an, Surah al-Hajj (22), verse 28.

of God, while concurrently refreshes our spirits, enabling us to find our purpose in life and focus on it. Nonetheless, God being Omnipresent allows His servants to understand and connect with Him wherever they are, without necessarily going to His House if they cannot afford it. Furthermore, Prophet Muhammad directed his community to attend the Friday prayers for those who could not afford the pilgrimage, by saying: "The Friday prayers is the pilgrimage of the poor."

وَاللَّهُ سَمِيعٌ عَلِيمٌ

> And God is All-Hearing, All-Knowing.[12]

Although God is Omnipresent, Imminent, All-Hearing, and All-Seeing, many people argue that they do not feel His presence in their lives. People's inability to feel God's presence in their lives is hindered by many elements - amongst them are sins. The sins that human beings perform take them away from God. This is beautifully mentioned in a supplication by Imam Zain al-Abedeen, who taught it to a companion by the name of Abu Hamza al-Thumali:

اَنَّكَ لا تَحْتَجِبُ عَنْ خَلْقِكَ إلاّ اَنْ تَحْجُبَهُمُ الاْعمالُ دُونَكَ

> You are not veiled from Your creatures, but the creatures are veiled from you through their sins.

Sins that human beings commit have the ability to intercept human relations with God. The more people are attached to lower life and materialism, the more they will be pushed away from a spiritual relationship with God. Sins damage the human spiritual faculty and take away the feeling of the presence of God from one's heart. When a person's ability to free oneself from the shackles of bondage to one's lower desires are incapacitated by

---

[12] Qur'an, Surah al-Baqarah (2), verse 256.

sins, one is then unable to enjoy the sweetness of God's Grace. Nevertheless, the forgiveness of God is always available for the sinners, and He constantly reaches out for His servants through His Love and Mercy.

قُلْ يَٰعِبَادِىَ ٱلَّذِينَ أَسْرَفُوا۟ عَلَىٰٓ أَنفُسِهِمْ لَا تَقْنَطُوا۟ مِن رَّحْمَةِ ٱللَّهِ ۚ
إِنَّ ٱللَّهَ يَغْفِرُ ٱلذُّنُوبَ جَمِيعًا ۚ إِنَّهُۥ هُوَ ٱلْغَفُورُ ٱلرَّحِيمُ

> Say: "O My servants who have been prodigal to the detriment of their own soul! Do not despair of God's Mercy. Truly God forgives all sins. Truly He is the All-Forgiving, the All-Merciful."[13]

Infinity

Human life is finite. The day we are born, we are propelled into a forward and consistent motion towards the end of our lives; it is something we have no control over. We live our lives in between the day we are born, and the day we will die. In stark contrast to us, God has no date of birth nor a date of death, and since He was not created, He has no beginning nor any end.

هُوَ الْأَوَّلُ وَالْآخِرُ وَالظَّاهِرُ وَالْبَاطِنُ

> He is the First, and the Last, and the Outward, and the Inward.[14]

اللَّهُ لَا إِلَٰهَ إِلَّا هُوَ الْحَيُّ الْقَيُّومُ

> God, there is no god but He, the Ever-Living, the Self-Subsisting.[15]

---

13 Qur'an, Surah al-Zumar (39), verse 53.
14 Qur'an, Surah al-Hadeed (57), verse 3.
15 Qur'an, Surah al-Baqarah (2), verse 255.

How is it Possible that God was not Created?

God was not created, and He is simply beyond any kind of comparison with other creations. One cannot compare the creation of humankind with that of God. To further illustrate this idea, we need to examine the three types of existence within Islamic philosophical thinking:

1. **Impossible Existence** ***(Mumtani'ul Wujood)*** - This is a type of existence that cannot exist. An example of this is the Existence of Contradiction (*Ijtimu'l Naqidayn*). Two things which contradict one another cannot be at the same place at the exact same time. For instance, one cannot say that something is black and white at the same time. It is either black or white.
2. **Possible or Transient Existence** ***(Mumkin'ul Wujood)*** - A clear example of this existence are human beings. *Mumkin* means either something can happen or it cannot take place. God could have created me, or He could have not created me - and this applies to all other creatures as well. Therefore, everything and everyone in this universe is considered to be transient.
3. **Essential or Absolute Existence** ***(Wajib'ul Wujood)*** - The only one example of this existence is God. He was not created, and He has no beginning, nor any end. Unlike human beings, God is an Essential Existence. He is the source, and the cause of every creation in this entire universe. *Wajib'ul Wujood* also means that He is Self-Subsisting and does not need a creator, nor a sustainer; and because of this nature, He does not possess any matter. He is the only one in the universe that does not possess an embodiment.

Why do people have difficulty understanding that God is *Wajib'ul Wujood* - that He has no parents, no creator, no beginning, no end - and why do they keep repeating the question of who created God? The human mind is preoccupied by the idea that everything has a beginning and a creator, as this is what people witness all around them. Animals, plants, people, machines, instruments, and everything else that is *Mumkin'ul Wujood* has a beginning, an end, and a creator. This is why it is important to understand the previously explained concept of *Al-Waahadiyyah* in God's Essence. He is unlike any other thing in the universe - in not having been created, and not having a beginning or an end - and that is the Uniqueness of His Essence (see Surah al-Shura (42), verse 11; and Surah al-Ikhlaas (112), verse 4).

Everything in this universe is bounded and limited by time and space, except God. God is Limitless and Boundless; He is Eternal and Infinite. Every event in this universe is finite and restricted by time, therefore as time passes by, the event reaches its expiry. Philosophers argue that the limitation of all existence is associated with its oblivion (محدودية الموجود ملازمة للتلبس بالعدم), meaning that 'everything that exists has a limit and a term.' This term and limitation are equated with an expiration and requirement that it must come to an end (بالعدم التلبس) at some point in time.

The Qur'an reminds us that the limitation and restriction of any existence has a correlation with it eventually becoming void, and the vanishing of that entity:

مَا عِندَكُمْ يَنفَدُ وَمَا عِندَ ٱللَّهِ بَاقٍ

> That which is with you will come to an end, but that which is with God will subsist.[16]

[16] Qur'an, Surah al-Nahl (16), verse 96.

Everything that people possess will one day vanish - be it power, leadership, position, wealth, or property, to name a few. However, that which is with God will always continue, and it will have no term, nor limit. Surely it will never vanish. This is the contrast between what human beings possess and what God possesses, for God is Eternal. All events and phenomena in this universe have to vanish because of their own restrictions and limitations.

وَالشَّمْسُ تَجْرِي لِمُسْتَقَرٍّ لَّهَا ذَٰلِكَ تَقْدِيرُ الْعَزِيزِ الْعَلِيمِ

> And the sun runs to a dwelling place of its own. That is the decree of the All-Mighty, the All-Knowing.[17]

In this solar system, which has been estimated to be five billion years old, is there anything greater than the sun? Even the sun will cease to exist one day. It is in constant motion towards its final destination which is eternal termination. The entire universe will follow suit once the sun is terminated. All of these events will take place because of their limitations in time.

إِذَا الشَّمْسُ كُوِّرَتْ ۞ وَإِذَا النُّجُومُ انكَدَرَتْ

> When the sun is enfolded, and when the stars fade away.[18]

ذَٰلِكَ بِأَنَّ اللَّهَ هُوَ الْحَقُّ وَأَنَّ مَا يَدْعُونَ مِن دُونِهِ الْبَاطِلُ وَأَنَّ اللَّهَ هُوَ الْعَلِيُّ الْكَبِيرُ

> That is because God, He is the Truth, and whatsoever they call upon other than Him is false, and God is the Exalted, the Great.[19]

---

[17] Qur'an, Surah Yaseen (36), verse 38.
[18] Qur'an, Surah al-Takweer (81), verses 1-2.
[19] Qur'an, Surah Luqmaan (31), verse 30.

While everything else in this universe will vanish, God is the only Truth and only Reality which will never disappear.

كُلُّ شَيْءٍ هَالِكٌ إِلَّا وَجْهَهُ

> All things will perish, except His Face.[20]

كُلُّ مَنْ عَلَيْهَا فَانٍ ۝ وَيَبْقَىٰ وَجْهُ رَبِّكَ ذُو الْجَلَالِ وَالْإِكْرَام

> All that is upon the earth will pass away.[21] And there will remain the Face of your Lord, Possessor of Majesty and Bounty.[22]

No matter how much materialistic and non materialistic possessions a person may accumulate during one's life span, eventually it will all evanesce. No matter how hard one works, there is an expiration date for what one produces. The previous verse gives a beautiful message that if someone works for God, then the benefit of that work will stay with him forever. On the contrary, if a person works for oneself, then the value of that work will dissipate. Let us all learn how to work for God, and invest in our relationship with Him through monotheism, in order that we achieve success in this life and in the afterlife. As a common saying states:

ما كان لله ينمو

> Whatever is dedicated to God will flourish.

---

[20] Qur'an, Surah al-Qasas (28), verse 88.
[21] Qur'an, Surah al-Rahmaan (55), verse 26.
[22] Qur'an, Surah al-Rahmaan (55), verse 27.

5

Unity of God's Deeds (*Tawheed al-Af'aal*)

ٱللَّهُ خَـٰلِقُ كُلِّ شَىْءٍ ۖ وَهُوَ عَلَىٰ كُلِّ شَىْءٍ وَكِيلٌ

> God is the Creator of all things, and He is a Guardian over all things.[1]

[1] Qur'an, Surah al-Zumar (39), verse 62.

The Unity of Deeds (*Tawheed al-Af'aal*) entails that every action and motion in this universe is solely attributed to God, and that He is solely behind their occurrence. The main source of power, energy, influence, and motion in this universe is undoubtedly God. He is the Sole Influencer (المؤثر الوحيد في هذا الكون هو الله).

As the Primary Source, all actions in this universe take place with the permission of God; all other sources are secondary and are inoperable without the permission of the Almighty. He is the only entity that is Self-Subsisting and Absolutely Independent. Undoubtedly, nothing sustains Him, rather, He sustains everything in existence.

To better understand the concept of the Unity of Deeds, the principle of "cause and effect" (العلة والمعلول) must be understood. A prime illustration of this concept is the creation of the sun: God created the sun as He wanted to bestow light and heat upon His other creations. Therefore, the sun is the cause, while the light and the heat from it are its effects. To further illustrate this point, let us look at the example of fire. God created fire, which is the cause, and its effect is the heat. The entire universe is based on this principle of "cause and effect." God, who creates the cause, creates the effects of it as well (الذي خلق العلة أعطى الآثار لها).

Human beings often deem themselves to be independent. However, no one can be totally independent when a person depends on external factors such as food, drink, shelter, clothing, health, social life, education, etc., for one's survival. Ultimately, we and everything else in this universe are completely dependent on God, and all of the blessings that He bestows upon us. The Qur'an beautifully sums up this notion:

يَٰٓأَيُّهَا ٱلنَّاسُ أَنتُمُ ٱلْفُقَرَآءُ إِلَى ٱللَّهِ ۖ وَٱللَّهُ هُوَ ٱلْغَنِيُّ ٱلْحَمِيدُ

> O mankind! You are needful of God; while He is the Self-Sufficient, the Praised.[1]

The Prophet used to often recite the below phrase:

لَا حَوْلَ وَلَا قُوَّةَ إِلَّا بِٱللهِ ٱلْعَلِيِّ ٱلْعَظِيمِ

> There is no power, nor strength except in God, the Lofty, the Great.

A created being does not have any power or authority other than what the Creator bestows upon it. One cannot claim to have innate power, guidance, or salvation except that which God has bestowed upon him. God is the source of all power, guidance, and salvation, for all creatures.

كُلًّا نُّمِدُّ هَٰٓؤُلَآءِ وَهَٰٓؤُلَآءِ مِنْ عَطَآءِ رَبِّكَ ۚ وَمَا كَانَ عَطَآءُ رَبِّكَ مَحْظُورًا

> Each do We aid - both these and those - with the gift of your Lord; and the gift of your Lord is not confined.[2]

Agents of God

God does not associate Himself with any partners, and His Efficacy knows none other than Him. However, He does have agents who execute His Commands. Even though He does not require any help in creating and sustaining the universe and everything within it, He uses spiritual agents, such as angels, to execute His Affairs. Furthermore, God's agents may come in the form of both human and material agents. By way of illustration,

---

[1] Qur'an, Surah Faatir (35), verse 15.
[2] Qur'an, Surah al-Isra (17), verse 20.

a doctor cannot cure a patient without the help of God, for doctors are completely dependent on God. It is solely with the permission and will of God that a doctor is able to cure patients.

A common question that is asked is that if God is the only entity that bestows power and strength, then why do angels execute His affairs? In the Qur'an it says:

فَٱلْمُدَبِّرَٰتِ أَمْرًا

> And by those (angels) that govern affairs.[3]

مَّا يَلْفِظُ مِن قَوْلٍ إِلَّا لَدَيْهِ رَقِيبٌ عَتِيدٌ

> No word does a person utter without a ready watcher beside them.[4]

The executors of God's will are the angels. They watch over all of creation and report directly to God. Furthermore, every single action we perform will be shown to us on the Day of Judgment through these angels.

Assuredly, God is Omnipotent, thus He did not create the angels to help Him, rather He created them to emphasize and reinforce the aforementioned principle of "cause and effect." Although God is capable of providing for and taking care of the entire universe directly Himself, it comes through means and intermediaries.

Angels have been commissioned by God to govern the affairs of the universe. However, it must be understood that their management is not done by their own power and will, but that of God.

---

[3] Qur'an, Surah al-Naaziat (79), verse 5.
[4] Qur'an, Surah Qaaf (50), verse 18.

ثُمَّ ٱسْتَوَىٰ عَلَى ٱلْعَرْشِ

> Then He (God) mounted the Throne.[5]

Metaphorically, God sits on His Throne, thus the absolute management of the universe only belongs to Him, and all of the angels execute God's will with His permission.

ٱللَّهُ خَـٰلِقُ كُلِّ شَىْءٍ ۖ وَهُوَ عَلَىٰ كُلِّ شَىْءٍ وَكِيلٌ

> God is the Creator of all things, and He is the Guardian over all things.[6]

God is the Creator, the Manager, and the Director of every single thing in this universe - no matter how small or big - and to Him belongs all power.

لَّهُۥ مَقَالِيدُ ٱلسَّمَـٰوَٰتِ وَٱلْأَرْضِ

> Unto Him belong the keys of the heavens and the earth.[7]

The above verses assert that God, without any partner or aid, is the Commander of the entire universe. Thus, He is the only entity who can help us when we need help. He is the only Sovereign Power in this universe, and all other powers and beings in this universe are subservient to Him, and cannot function without His permission. Every power is derived from and generated by Him.

Is God Responsible for Man's Bad Behaviors?

We have established that God is the Generator of every motion in this universe, be it good or bad. However, this does not mean that He consents to evil acts or any kind of injustice. Although

---

[5] Qur'an, Surah al-A'raaf (7), verse 54.
[6] Qur'an, Surah al-Zumar (39), verse 62.
[7] Qur'an, Surah al-Shura (42), verse 12.

oppressive acts like murder, rape, physical abuse, and all other types of aggression can only be generated through power and energy provided by God to mankind, they are not consented, nor condoned by God; for God does not excuse injustice for humankind.

To simplify this concept, one may use the example of a father who provides provision for his family. While some members of his family will make good use of the money that he gives to them, others may misuse it. Although the father is the source of the financial aid, he does not agree to the mishandling of his money. Likewise, God provides man with free will, freedom of choice, and guidance to know what is right and wrong, but does not interfere in their daily decisions. Rather God holds people accountable for the decisions they make. If man insists on violating His rules and does not seek repentance, then surely he will be held accountable for his misdeeds. If God were to dictate or control everyone's actions, then there would be no merit for anyone, nor any value or need for free will.

One must understand that while God has given man free will, the way a person uses it is one's own choice, and God must not be blamed for the negative results that people's poor choices may bring about. The free will that God bestows on a person is meant to be used to build oneself and the society, not to become a source of destruction. Some people use their free will to heed God's call and help their societies, while others choose to go down the path of destruction.

مَّنْ عَمِلَ صَٰلِحًا فَلِنَفْسِهِۦ ۖ وَمَنْ أَسَآءَ فَعَلَيْهَا ۗ وَمَا رَبُّكَ بِظَلَّٰمٍ لِّلْعَبِيدِ

> Whosoever works righteousness, it is for one's own soul. And whosoever commits evil, it is to the detriment thereof. It is not for your Lord to wrong His servants.[8]

Be it physical or spiritual, God asserts that every action which is taken, will have a reaction. If a person uses one's free will to commit an evil deed, then it will be to one's own detriment. However, if an individual uses one's free will to walk down the path of obedience and surrender to God, then that person will be the benefactor of those good acts both in this world and in the hereafter. It is those people who will enjoy the internal peace and satisfaction.

Imam Ali once said: "I have never done any goodness to any person in my life." The listeners were somewhat bewildered, as the Imam had dedicated his entire life to doing good to others. He then eloquently referred to the Qur'anic verse:

إِنْ أَحْسَنتُمْ أَحْسَنتُمْ لِأَنفُسِكُمْ ۖ

> If you are virtuous, then you are virtuous for the sake of your own souls.[9]

Does God Have a Role in Preventing Evil?

إِنَّا خَلَقْنَا ٱلْإِنسَٰنَ مِن نُّطْفَةٍ أَمْشَاجٍ نَّبْتَلِيهِ فَجَعَلْنَٰهُ سَمِيعًۢا بَصِيرًا ۝ إِنَّا هَدَيْنَٰهُ ٱلسَّبِيلَ إِمَّا شَاكِرًا وَإِمَّا كَفُورًا

[8] Qur'an, Surah Fussilat (41), verse 46.
[9] Qur'an, Surah al-Isra (17), verse 7.

> Truly We created man from a drop of mixed fluid that We may test him, and We endowed him with hearing, seeing. Truly We guided him upon the way, be he grateful or ungrateful.[10]

When God created man, He intended guidance and salvation for them. As such, He continuously provides people with every physical and spiritual venue to attain guidance. Mankind is shown the right path by God, and He gives them the tools to distinguish it from the wrong path. He further invites and encourages man to follow the right way and avoid the wrong ones. However, it is a man's own choice as to which path he wants to follow. One might ask why God does not force everyone to go down the right path. In response, it is incumbent to recognise that coercion is against God's will, for He does not want anyone to follow the right path through force; rather He wants people to do so through conviction, understanding, and love. This is the only way to enjoy the sweetness of faith and nearness to God.

One of the most basic fundamentals of Islamic faith is the concept of non-coercion, which has been mentioned in the second chapter of the Qur'an.

لَآ إِكۡرَاهَ فِي ٱلدِّينِۖ

> There is no coercion in religion.[11]

The inseparability of love and faith means that the former plays a pivotal role in embracing one's faith. When it comes to practicing religion, neither force, nor intimidation and fear can ensure the continuity of one's practice; it is love that makes a person follow the religious teachings. An individual has to love

---

[10] Qur'an, Surah al-Insaan (76), verses 2-3.
[11] Qur'an, Surah al-Baqarah (2), verse 256.

the acts of worship such as prayers, fasting, and almsgiving, in order to enjoy their fruits. Religion should be followed with love, for it is only through love that we can remain true to our convictions. The concept of hijab serves as an example of love. What makes one group of Muslim women observe the hijab, while others do not? It is only the conviction and appreciation of an individual belief that makes the hijab worthy. Otherwise, if hijab is forced upon a woman, then not only will she not enjoy observing it, she will furthermore see it as a burden and defy it. One should love the hijab, then she will observe and defend it.

Some people ask the following: "If God is the source of every power and action in this universe, and He is all Merciful, then why is there so much injustice? Why does poverty exist? Why do pandemics happen? Why do wars break out?" The Qur'an emphasises that evil actions and injustices on the earth are people's own doings, and that God never intends mischief or oppression against His people.

ظَهَرَ ٱلْفَسَادُ فِى ٱلْبَرِّ وَٱلْبَحْرِ بِمَا كَسَبَتْ أَيْدِى ٱلنَّاسِ لِيُذِيقَهُم بَعْضَ ٱلَّذِى عَمِلُوا۟ لَعَلَّهُمْ يَرْجِعُونَ

> Corruption has appeared on land and sea because of that which men's hands have earned, that He may let them taste some of that which they have done, that haply they might return.[12]

God will never impose His will upon us. He has given us free will, so we may use it responsibly for our own salvation. The Qur'anic principle mentioned above of "no coercion in matters of faith" means that God wants the best of His creations - human beings - to willfully believe and embrace His directives and

[12] Qur'an, Surah al-Room (30), verse 41.

execute them so that they may stay true to their conviction. However, it must be stressed that He does not abandon anyone because they have free will, or if they make a poor choice. God is always present and available to help; and He intervenes as He wills to save, protect, and guide His servants.

When it comes to free will, it must be noted that human beings are the only creation of God who have this free will. It is what distinguishes human beings from animals, who do not possess free will and , therefore, do not bear responsibilities for their actions. Human beings, on the other hand, will be held accountable for their actions, since they have the free will to commit different actions. A person is free to choose whatever path to follow. This is why some people drift away from faith despite them being born into practicing families. In the same way, there are people who choose to come to Islam despite them being born in non-Muslim families. If God had not given human beings free will, and instead He was responsible for the actions that they commit, then there would be no reason for testing humanity in this lifetime.

Ash'arites (Coercionists), argue against the free will of human beings; for them, it is God who engineers and directs a person's choice and actions. However, one must understand that there is a fine line between God guiding people, and Him controlling them.

إِنَّا هَدَيْنَٰهُ ٱلسَّبِيلَ

> Truly We guided him upon the way, be he grateful or ungrateful.[13]

[13] Qur'an, Surah al-Insaan (76), verse 3.

أَلَمْ نَجْعَل لَّهُۥ عَيْنَيْنِ ۝ وَلِسَانًا وَشَفَتَيْنِ ۝ وَهَدَيْنَٰهُ ٱلنَّجْدَيْنِ

> Did We not make for him two eyes, and a tongue, and two lips, and guide him upon the two ways?[14]

God's guidance is synonymous with His help, not His control. Coercionists believe that God controls everything that a person does. For example, if someone commits an evil deed, then it is because God determined for this person to commit such a wrongdoing. This would mean that eternal damnation is already decided for people because God chose that for them. However, the Qur'an clearly states otherwise:

إِنَّ ٱللَّهَ لَا يَأْمُرُ بِٱلْفَحْشَآءِ ۖ أَتَقُولُونَ عَلَى ٱللَّهِ مَا لَا تَعْلَمُونَ

> "Truly God commands not indecency. Do you say of God that which you know not?"[15]

God is Just, and never goes against His own law.

According to Coercionists, God created two types of people: those who do good (as per God's coercion) so that they can be taken to heaven, and those who do evil (as per God's coercion) so that they can be taken to hell. This is not compatible with God's Justice and Mercy.

God has sent messengers, scriptures, and books for mankind so that man may use free will to be guided by them, and so that no one on the Day of Judgment can claim that they were not informed.

---

[14] Qur'an, Surah al-Balad (90), verses 8-10.
[15] Qur'an, Surah al-A'raaf (7), verse 28.

لِئَلَّا يَكُونَ لِلنَّاسِ عَلَى ٱللَّهِ حُجَّةٌۢ بَعْدَ ٱلرُّسُلِ

> So that mankind might have no argument against God after the messengers.[16]

God sent many reminders to awaken man's conscience, so that man may make the right decisions and follow His Path. Man's free will is an incentive for him. It shows him that the more he does good, the more he will be rewarded. God says in the Qur'an:

وَأَن لَّيْسَ لِلْإِنسَـٰنِ إِلَّا مَا سَعَىٰ ۝ وَأَنَّ سَعْيَهُۥ سَوْفَ يُرَىٰ ۝
ثُمَّ يُجْزَىٰهُ ٱلْجَزَآءَ ٱلْأَوْفَىٰ

> And that man shall have nothing but that for which he endeavored, and that his endeavoring shall be seen, whereupon he will be rewarded for it with the fullest reward.[17]

The Guardianship and Protection of God encompasses all of His beings - regardless of whether they believe in Him or not. One might ask how it is possible that God bestows His Mercy and Blessings upon those who do not follow Him? God is the Lord of the entire universe, not merely the Lord of an elite group of humans. For Him, all creatures are His people and dependents, and He must sustain and provide for them all - regardless of whether they believe in Him or not. In this life, each individual will receive their portion of provision and help from God, whereas in the hereafter, those who followed God's Path will be rewarded by Him.

---

16 Qur'an, Surah al-Nisaa (4), verse 165.
17 Qur'an, Surah al-Najm (53), verses 39-41.

لِإِيلَٰفِ قُرَيْشٍ ۝ إِۦلَٰفِهِمْ رِحْلَةَ ٱلشِّتَآءِ وَٱلصَّيْفِ ۝ فَلْيَعْبُدُوا۟
رَبَّ هَٰذَا ٱلْبَيْتِ ۝ ٱلَّذِىٓ أَطْعَمَهُم مِّن جُوعٍ وَءَامَنَهُم مِّنْ خَوْفٍۭ

> For the secure passage of the Quraysh, their secure passage in the journey of winter and of summer; so let them worship the Lord of this House, Who relieved them of hunger, and made them safe from fear.[18]

Despite the idol worshipping of the Quraysh, God still provided them with their basic necessities.

When it comes to God's Guidance however, He can bestow it upon whomever He wills. It must be noted that there are two stages of guidance:

1. General guidance that God bestows upon each and every one of His creations, as He mentions in the Qur'an:

إِنَّا هَدَيْنَٰهُ ٱلسَّبِيلَ إِمَّا شَاكِرًا وَإِمَّا كَفُورًا

> Truly We guided him upon the way, be he grateful or ungrateful.[19]

قَالَ رَبُّنَا ٱلَّذِىٓ أَعْطَىٰ كُلَّ شَىْءٍ خَلْقَهُۥ ثُمَّ هَدَىٰ

> He said: "Our Lord is He Who gives everything its creation, then guides [it]."[20]

2. Special guidance that God bestows only upon those people who are willing to follow His Path.

---

[18] Qur'an, Surah Quraysh (106), verses 1-4.
[19] Qur'an, Surah al-Insaan (76), verse 3.
[20] Qur'an, Surah Taha (20), verse 50.

وَٱلَّذِينَ ٱهْتَدَوْا۟ زَادَهُمْ هُدًى وَءَاتَىٰهُمْ تَقْوَىٰهُمْ

> And those who accept guidance, He increases them in guidance, and grants them their reverence.[21]

وَيَزِيدُ ٱللَّهُ ٱلَّذِينَ ٱهْتَدَوْا۟ هُدًى ۗ

> And God increases in guidance those who are rightly guided.[22]

God's Guidance is integral to the survival of everything in and out of the universe. Our relationship with God resembles an infant's relationship with one's parents; oftentimes, we do not recognize the connection we have with God, but His Guidance is always with us. An infant may not realize that his mother is always guarding him against danger; similarly, those who do not believe in God do not realize that He is the One who is providing and protecting them so they can carry out their responsibilities.

لَوْ يُؤَاخِذُ ٱللَّهُ ٱلنَّاسَ بِمَا كَسَبُوا۟ مَا تَرَكَ عَلَىٰ ظَهْرِهَا مِن دَآبَّةٍ
وَلَـٰكِن يُؤَخِّرُهُمْ إِلَىٰٓ أَجَلٍ مُّسَمًّى ۖ فَإِذَا جَآءَ أَجَلُهُمْ فَإِنَّ ٱللَّهَ كَانَ
بِعِبَادِهِۦ بَصِيرًۢا

> Were God to take mankind to task for that which they have earned, He would not leave a single creature upon it (the surface of the earth). But He grants them reprieve until a term appointed. And when their term comes, truly God sees His servants.[23]

---

[21] Qur'an, Surah Muhammad (47), verse 17.
[22] Qur'an, Surah Maryam (19), verse 76.
[23] Qur'an, Surah Faatir (35), verse 45.

God mentions in the Qur'an that He has "prescribed Mercy for Himself."[24] He promised to provide guidance, provision, and protection to all of His creatures - indiscriminately. Everyone, regardless of their failures, deserves to be given a second, third, or fourth chance, and so on. God's policy is not to punish people immediately for their sins and wrongdoings; rather He gives them time and respite to go back to Him and seek forgiveness for their shortcomings.

There is an interesting story about a famous champion wrestler who came to the arena one day for his event. Before the start of the match, some of his fans were telling him to ask God for help against his powerful opponent, but he strongly refused. His hubris saw him proclaim: "No power in this universe, including God, will be able to defeat me." In his mind, he was well-prepared to defeat his opponent. He had won many championships before, so he believed that there was no reason to ask for God's help, as he could handle it by himself. In the first round of his match, he was able to overcome his opponent, but later on his opponent knocked him down, and he sustained serious injuries to the brain; he was immediately transferred to a hospital. He was visited several times in the hospital by his fans, but as time went on, people started to forget about him, and he was abandoned. When he eventually died, he was alone in the hospital. It is interesting to note that the person who stood in the ring with so much arrogance that he started to defy God, was the same person who then laid down paralyzed on a hospital bed, not even able to move a muscle.

---

[24] Qur'an, Surah al-An'aam (6), verse 54.

قُلْ مَن ذَا ٱلَّذِى يَعْصِمُكُم مِّنَ ٱللَّهِ إِنْ أَرَادَ بِكُمْ سُوٓءًا أَوْ أَرَادَ
بِكُمْ رَحْمَةً ۚ وَلَا يَجِدُونَ لَهُم مِّن دُونِ ٱللَّهِ وَلِيًّا وَلَا نَصِيرًا

> Say: "Who is it who will protect you from God if He desires evil for you or desires mercy for you?" They will find no protector or helper for themselves apart from God.[25]

Having all of the world's wealth and strength does not make a person self-sufficient. Only God is Self-Sufficient, and every single thing depends on Him.

The consequences of man's deeds - whether good or bad, right or wrong - are not limited to this life only. Everyone will continue to see the results of one's actions in the hereafter as well. Man will be shown all the choices he made - positive and negative; and on the Day of Judgment, these choices will decide one's ultimate fate.

وَكُلَّ إِنسَـٰنٍ أَلْزَمْنَـٰهُ طَـٰٓئِرَهُۥ فِى عُنُقِهِۦ

> And [for] every man We have fastened his omen upon his neck.[26]

Prophet Muhammad taught that if one wishes to know whether he would have eternal blessings or eternal damnation in the afterlife, then he should analyze how he is spending life in this world.

إنكم تحشرون كما حييتم في هذه الدنيا

> You will be resurrected the way that you lived in this life.

Prophet Muhammad taught that if one leads a life of honesty, piety, and righteousness, then one does not need to worry about

---

[25] Qur'an, Surah al-Ahzaab (33), verse 17.
[26] Qur'an, Surah al-Isra (17), verse 13.

failure in the hereafter. However, if one chooses to lead a life of sins and transgressions, then there will be dire consequences.

بَلِ ٱلْإِنسَٰنُ عَلَىٰ نَفْسِهِۦ بَصِيرَةٌ

> Indeed, man shall be a testimony against himself.[27]

God has gifted man with inner-conscience and reason to enable him to realize what is right and what is wrong.

وَلَآ أُقْسِمُ بِٱلنَّفْسِ ٱللَّوَّامَةِ

> And I swear by the self-accusing soul.[28]

This inner-conscience is God's Mercy towards His people, for He does not want man to suffer eternal damnation. Free will takes man to a higher level of moral integrity. Spiritual perfection would imminently be out of reach without free will, since there would not be any struggle in life. Struggle is necessary to reach the summit of perfection; and a lack of struggle will result in a lack of destination. When there is no pain, there will definitely be no gain - be it in worldly affairs or spiritual ones. God outlines this in the Qur'an:

يَٰٓأَيُّهَا ٱلْإِنسَٰنُ إِنَّكَ كَادِحٌ إِلَىٰ رَبِّكَ كَدْحًا فَمُلَٰقِيهِ

> O mankind! Truly you are laboring towards your Lord laboriously, and shall meet Him![29]

The stance of the school of the Prophet and his progeny on the issue of coercion and free will has been affirmed by the sayings of Imam Jafar al-Sadiq:

---

[27] Qur'an, Surah al-Qiyaamah (75), verse 14.
[28] Qur'an, Surah al-Qiyaamah (75), verse 2.
[29] Qur'an, Surah al-Inshiqaaq (84), verse 6.

لا جبر ولا تفويض وإنما أمر بين أمرين

> "There is neither absolute force, nor absolute free will. Rather, a matter between the two."[30]

No absolute coercion, nor an absolute free will exists when it comes to our lives. It must be understood that free will does not mean having complete freedom. There are certain things which God has already chosen for us, such as: our parents, our date and place of birth, our time and place of death, our ethnicity, etc. However, it is not these factors that determine our fate.

إِنَّ ٱلْإِنسَـٰنَ لَفِى خُسْرٍ ۝ إِلَّا ٱلَّذِينَ ءَامَنُوا۟ وَعَمِلُوا۟ ٱلصَّـٰلِحَـٰتِ

> Truly mankind is in loss, except those who believe, and perform righteous deeds.[31]

Man's belief and actions determine our fate and make the final decision for us in the afterlife.

[30] *Bihaar al-Anwaar*, Al-Majlisi, vol. 75, pg. 354.
[31] Qur'an, Surah al-Asr (103), verses 2-3.

6

Unity of Worshipping God (*Tawheed al-Ibaadah*)

وَمَآ أُمِرُوٓاْ إِلَّا لِيَعۡبُدُواْ ٱللَّهَ مُخۡلِصِينَ لَهُ ٱلدِّينَ حُنَفَآءَ وَيُقِيمُواْ
ٱلصَّلَوٰةَ وَيُؤۡتُواْ ٱلزَّكَوٰةَۚ وَذَٰلِكَ دِينُ ٱلۡقَيِّمَةِ

> They were not commanded but to worship God, devoting religion entirely to Him, as upright *(hanif)*, and to establish the prayer, and to give the alms - that is the upright religion.[1]

[1] Qur'an, Surah al-Bayyinah (98), verse 5.

The fourth dimension of monotheism is *Tawheed al-Ibaadah,* the Unity of the Worshipping of God. This is the most important dimension of monotheism. God states in the Qur'an:

وَمَآ أَرْسَلْنَا مِن قَبْلِكَ مِن رَّسُولٍ إِلَّا نُوحِىٓ إِلَيْهِ أَنَّهُۥ لَآ إِلَٰهَ إِلَّآ أَنَا۠ فَٱعْبُدُونِ

> And We sent no messenger before you except that We revealed to him: "Verily, there is no god but I; so worship Me!"[1]

The only entity in this universe that is worthy of being worshipped is God. To worship anything besides God, or alongside God, is an act of blasphemy. A devout man should dedicate his entire life to God, as Prophet Abraham said:

قُلْ إِنَّ صَلَاتِى وَنُسُكِى وَمَحْيَاىَ وَمَمَاتِى لِلَّهِ رَبِّ ٱلْعَٰلَمِينَ

> Say: "Truly my prayer and my sacrifice, my living and my dying are all for God, Lord of the worlds.[2]

لَا شَرِيكَ لَهُۥ ۖ وَبِذَٰلِكَ أُمِرْتُ وَأَنَا۠ أَوَّلُ ٱلْمُسْلِمِينَ

> "He has no partner. This I am commanded, and I am the first of those who submit."[3]

Prophet Abraham serves as a paradigm of absolute dedication to God. The essence of this kind of dedication is the quality of earnestness (*ikhlaas*). Sincerity and dedication to God should be one's ultimate goal in all aspects of life - be it in praying, giving charity, working hard in school, or being a good person.

---

1 Qur'an, Surah al-Anbiya (21), verse 25.
2 Qur'an, Surah al-An'aam (6), verse 162.
3 Qur'an, Surah al-An'aam (6), verse 163.

Like Prophet Abraham, Prophet Joseph was also exceptionally dedicated to God. He is described in the Qur'an as being chosen by God:

إِنَّهُۥ مِنْ عِبَادِنَا ٱلْمُخْلَصِينَ

> Truly he was among Our chosen servants.[4]

Even in the most critical moments in his life, Prophet Joseph never let his heart get attached to anything other than God. This is the highest level of servitude, earnestness, and dedication to the Almighty God.

What Constitutes an Act of Worship?

The true nature of worship has been a topic of intense discussion among Muslim theologians for a very long time. Some consider visiting a grave as an act of worship, while others believe that to ask a dead *wali* for help, bow down to a person as a sign of respect, and to kiss an object out of reverence are acts of blasphemy. Even touching the wall of the Ka'bah for blessings is an act of blasphemy for some.

The School of the *Ahlulbayt* states that there is a fine line between an act of worship and an act of reverence. Not every act of reverence is necessarily an act of worship. The School of the *Ahlulbayt* emphasises the rational and intellectual approach in understanding religion; meaning that faith follows intellect. Every narration is examined through reason, while much importance is given to juristic reasoning (*ijtihaad*). Scholars spend many years studying to reach the level of juristic reasoning, and depend on reason and intelligence to extract Islamic rulings from the Qur'an and the Sunnah, the primary sources.

---

[4] Qur'an, Surah Yusuf (12), verse 24.

The bowing of a student before one's teacher as a sign of respect, the kissing of a parent's hand, or the kissing of a loved one's grave are not acts of real worship. One could excessively admire and love another being and even verbally state to "worship" him or her, yet still it is religiously not considered an act of real worship, nor does it mean that the individual is drifting away from the course of monotheism. On the other hand, if one follows another person or an object, believing that it is a source of spiritual guidance independent from God, then that act is considered to be worship. Therefore, one has to be very attentive and careful when discussing the nuances of the aspects of monotheism. What does the Qur'an say about this?

If we look at chapter 36 of the Qur'an, we see the word *ibaadah* being used there. It must be noted that the word *ibaadah* there does not mean worshipping. In Arabic literature, it is common to use the word *ibaadah* to show obedience, love, or respect towards someone or something.

أَلَمْ أَعْهَدْ إِلَيْكُمْ يَـٰبَنِىٓ ءَادَمَ أَن لَّا تَعْبُدُوا۟ ٱلشَّيْطَـٰنَ ۖ إِنَّهُۥ لَكُمْ
عَدُوٌّ مُّبِينٌ ۝ وَأَنِ ٱعْبُدُونِى ۚ هَـٰذَا صِرَٰطٌ مُّسْتَقِيمٌ

> Did I not enjoin upon you, O Children of Adam that you not worship [obey] Satan - truly he is a manifest enemy unto you and that you worship Me? This is a straight path.[5]

In the above verse, the word *ta'bodo* (which is a derivative of *ibaadah)* is used to warn people against obeying Satan, and how they must not worship him. The Qur'an illustrates that obeying Satan is equal to worshipping him.

---

[5] Qur'an, Surah Yaseen (36), verses 60-61.

Three Definitions of Worship

Regarding the use of the word *ibaadah*, scholars have come up with three different definitions to help explain the true meaning of it. These three definitions are studied nowadays to distinguish between worship and acts of love and respect.

1. **The first definition of *ibaadah*** is a form of verbal and physical submission to someone or something with the belief in its divinity. For example, if one goes to a tree and verbally or physically bows before that tree, and at the same time believes in the divinity of that said tree, then this is a form of blasphemy.

If one submits oneself to someone or something without believing in the divinity of that said person or thing, then this is not considered to be an act of worship, but may be an act of love and respect. If one claims that someone is a servant of a Prophet or an Imam and addresses him as a master, but does not believe that he carries any Lordship in any form or shape, then this is not an act of blasphemy.

The Qur'an mentions a story of Prophet Abraham with his uncle:

وَإِذْ قَالَ إِبْرَٰهِيمُ لِأَبِيهِ ءَازَرَ أَتَتَّخِذُ أَصْنَامًا ءَالِهَةً إِنِّيٓ أَرَىٰكَ
وَقَوْمَكَ فِي ضَلَٰلٍ مُّبِينٍ

> And when Abraham said unto his father, Azar: "Do you take idols for gods? Truly I see you and your people in manifest error."[6]

In Arabic literature, it is customary to address one's teacher or nurturer as a father. In this verse, Prophet Abraham is speaking to his uncle, Azar, and accuses him and his community of committing blasphemy, because they took the idols as their lords

[6] Qur'an, Surah al-An'aam (6), verse 74.

and bowed down before them believing in their divinity. The Qur'an also explains in the chapter of Mary:

وَٱتَّخَذُواْ مِن دُونِ ٱللَّهِ ءَالِهَةً لِّيَكُونُواْ لَهُمۡ عِزًّا

> And they have taken apart from God (false) deities that they might be a strength for them.[7]

The polytheists did not take idols to worship with the intention to respect them, but rather with the intention to believe in their divinity and supernatural powers.

Demonstrating reverence for a statute or a certain item is considered an act of *ibaadah*, or blasphemy, only if that reverence is accompanied by the belief in the divinity of that statue or item. However, if that reverence is not accompanied by the belief in the divinity of that statue or item, then it is not an act of blasphemy.

The Qur'an speaks about the polytheists in the previous verse and how they asked their idols for glory and power. In this case, the worshipping of the idols by the polytheists was an act of blasphemy, as they took their idols as their lords and begged them to grant them glory and power.

However, it is completely acceptable to ask a Prophet or an Imam for any kind of lawful help and intercession. This is not considered an act of blasphemy because there is no belief in the lordship or divinity of the Prophet or Imam.

2. The second definition of *ibaadah* is to submit oneself to a person or an object with the belief that the said person or object has full control independently from God. This is an act of blasphemy, because it is only God who has full control over us.

---

[7] Qur'an, Surah Maryam (19), verse 81.

يَٰٓأَيُّهَا ٱلنَّاسُ ٱعْبُدُوا۟ رَبَّكُمُ ٱلَّذِى خَلَقَكُمْ وَٱلَّذِينَ مِن قَبْلِكُمْ

> O mankind! Worship your Lord Who created you, and those who were before you.[8]

ٱللَّهُ ٱلَّذِى خَلَقَكُمْ ثُمَّ رَزَقَكُمْ ثُمَّ يُمِيتُكُمْ ثُمَّ يُحْيِيكُمْ

> God it is Who created you, then nourished you, then He will cause you to die, then He will give you life.[9]

These two verses from the Qur'an emphasize the full control that only God has over us, in all aspects of our lives. To give this authority to someone or something else besides God is an act of blasphemy. However, to ask a Prophet or an Imam for help while acknowledging the fact that they do not have full control over our lives, but that they act as intercessors between us and God, and can only fulfill our requests with God's permission, is not an act of blasphemy at all.

3. The third definition of *ibaadah* is to submit oneself to a person or an object believing that the said person or object is self-sufficient and self-subsisting. This is an act of blasphemy. No one in this universe is self-sufficient or self-subsisting except for God; everything else in existence depends on Him.

ٱللَّهُ لَآ إِلَٰهَ إِلَّا هُوَ ٱلْحَىُّ ٱلْقَيُّومُ

> God, there is no deity but He, the Ever-Living, the Self-Subsisting.[10]

While everything and everyone depends on God, this theory is not reciprocal, for God is independent of anything or anyone.

[8] Qur'an, Surah al-Baqarah (2), verse 21.
[9] Qur'an, Surah al-Room (30), verse 40.
[10] Qur'an, Surah al-Baqarah (2), verse 255.

Going to the Prophet or the Imams to seek their intercession is not an act of blasphemy because neither of them are self-sufficient or self-subsisting. They are the gateways to God. In Christian theology, Jesus is described as the Lord, while in Islamic theology, the Prophets and the Imams are described as a way to the Lord.

It must be noted that although both Christians and Muslims believe that Jesus performed miracles, they both differ greatly in how the miracles were performed. Christians believe that Jesus performed miracles because he is the Lord, Muslims believe that Jesus performed miracles because God provided him with the ability to do so. (further elaborated in Chapter 8)

Reverence versus Worship

Not every act of respect and love equates to worshipping. We have established that loving the Prophets or the Imams, and asking them for intercession, does not equate to worshipping them; one must only worship God. Prophets and Imams represent the path to God.

يَٰٓأَيُّهَا ٱلَّذِينَ ءَامَنُوا۟ ٱتَّقُوا۟ ٱللَّهَ وَكُونُوا۟ مَعَ ٱلصَّٰدِقِينَ

> O you who believe! Have God-consciousness, and be among the truthful ones.[11]

The Prophets and Imams help us in getting closer to God because they lived their lives as honest and truthful individuals. Therefore, visiting their shrines and paying respect to them are not acts of blasphemy, rather they are acts that bring us closer to God.

There is a difference between the linguistic meaning of worshipping and the spiritual one. Arabic dictionaries such as

---

[11] Qur'an, Surah al-Tawbah (9), verse 119.

Lisan al-Arab (by Ibn Manzur), *Al-Qamous* (by Firouzabadi), and *Al-Mufradat* (by Al-Raghib al-Isfahani) use three words to describe worship: submission, humility, and obedience. But even these three terms do not necessarily equate to spiritually worshiping someone or something. For example, we may submit and humble ourselves before our elders, but this does not mean that we are worshipping them. Another example is obedience in the military. The soldiers of an army salute or bow down to the commanders to express submission and obedience, but this is not in the sense of worshipping them.

Bowing to someone or something is considered an act of worship if it is done with the belief in the divinity of that said person or object, and thinking that they can independently answer prayers, grant wishes, or have full control over our lives. This being said, there are no intelligent Muslims who seek help from Prophet Muhammad or his progeny with the belief in their divinity. Believers seek help from them knowing that they are servants of God, depend entirely on God, and can only fulfill any requests by the permission of God. They go to them knowing that they were sent as a mercy from God to mankind.

"Grave worshipper" is a term invented by a cult that accuses others of blasphemy for seeking help from the Prophet when visiting his grave in Medina. This cult does not have its claim backed by the Qur'an. The Prophet himself used to visit the graves to pay tribute to the deceased, pray for them, and seek forgiveness on their behalf. It must be noted that no one in their right mind, would spend a lump sum of money to go to Mecca or Medina just to worship the graves there! Unfortunately, not using one's intellect leads to intolerance, ignorance, and name-calling.

فَسَجَدَ ٱلۡمَلَٰٓئِكَةُ كُلُّهُمۡ أَجۡمَعُونَ ۝ إِلَّآ إِبۡلِيسَ أَبَىٰٓ أَن يَكُونَ مَعَ ٱلسَّٰجِدِينَ

> Thereupon the angels prostrated, all of them together, except Iblīs. He refused to be with those who prostrated.[12]

When God created Prophet Adam, He commanded all of the angels to prostrate before him and they did, except for Satan (Iblis). The prostration of the angels before Adam was not an act of heresy, rather it was an act of obedience towards God because the angels did what God commanded them to do. Everyone prostrated down, except for Satan who argued:

قَالَ مَا مَنَعَكَ أَلَّا تَسۡجُدَ إِذۡ أَمَرۡتُكَۖ قَالَ أَنَا۠ خَيۡرٞ مِّنۡهُ خَلَقۡتَنِي مِن نَّارٖ وَخَلَقۡتَهُۥ مِن طِينٖ

> [God] said: "What prevented you from prostrating when I commanded you?" [Satan] said: "I am better than him. You created me from fire, while You created him from clay."[13]

It was Satan's arrogance, which was the first sin in this universe that caused his demotion and expulsion from heaven.

قَالَ فَٱهۡبِطۡ مِنۡهَا فَمَا يَكُونُ لَكَ أَن تَتَكَبَّرَ فِيهَا فَٱخۡرُجۡ إِنَّكَ مِنَ ٱلصَّٰغِرِينَ

> [God] said: "Get down from it! It is not for you to be arrogant here. So go forth! You are surely among those who are disgraced."[14]

---

[12] Qur'an, Surah al-Hijr (15), verses 30-31.
[13] Qur'an, Surah al-A'raaf (7), verse 12.
[14] Qur'an, Surah al-A'raaf (7), verse 13.

Another example of people prostrating to another person is that of Prophet Jacob and his family, when they were reunited with Prophet Joseph after forty years of separation.

وَرَفَعَ أَبَوَيْهِ عَلَى ٱلْعَرْشِ وَخَرُّواْ لَهُۥ سُجَّدًاۖ وَقَالَ يَٰٓأَبَتِ هَٰذَا تَأْوِيلُ رُءْيَٰيَ مِن قَبْلُ قَدْ جَعَلَهَا رَبِّي حَقًّا

> And he raised his parents upon the throne, and they [all] fell down in prostration towards him. And he said: "O my father! This is the fulfillment of my vision of before; my Lord has made it come true."[15]

When Prophet Joseph was finally reunited with his family, they fell down into prostration in front of him, something which Joseph had seen in a dream before and had mentioned to his father, Jacob.

يَٰٓأَبَتِ إِنِّي رَأَيْتُ أَحَدَ عَشَرَ كَوْكَبًا وَٱلشَّمْسَ وَٱلْقَمَرَ رَأَيْتُهُمْ لِي سَٰجِدِينَ

> "O my father, truly I have seen (in a dream) eleven stars, and the sun and the moon. I saw them prostrating to me."[16]

Was this an act of blasphemy on behalf of Jacob to prostrate before his son Joseph? As a Prophet, Jacob had full understanding about the meaning of blasphemy. He threw himself down into prostration in front of his son out of love, not because he believed that his son was divine.

A third example of people prostrating before a person or an object without the intention of worshipping them, is the act of standing behind the station of Abraham (*Maqaam Ibrahim*) in the

---

[15] Qur'an, Surah Yusuf (12), verse 100.
[16] Qur'an, Surah Yusuf (12), verse 4.

Sacred Mosque (*Masjid al-Haraam*) of Mecca to offer a prayer as part of the pilgrimage rites. God mentions this in the Qur'an:

وَٱتَّخِذُواْ مِن مَّقَامِ إِبْرَٰهِـۧمَ مُصَلًّى

> And take the station of Abraham as a place of prayer.[17]

Praying behind the station of Abraham is a gesture of acknowledgement and appreciation for the sacrifices that were made by him. This act does not constitute worshipping him. Likewise, bowing and prostrating in front of the Ka'bah does not mean that someone is worshipping it in any way whatsoever.

Another example of an act of respect is that which is shown to the Black Stone (*Hajr al-Aswad*), a revered object by the Muslims. It is believed that an angel standing next to it watches over the pilgrims who are performing circumambulation around the House of God. Those who touch and kiss the Black Stone are not doing so with the intention of worshipping it, but rather to show their respect and love, and to follow the tradition of Prophet Muhammad. With the same token, kissing the Qur'an and touching a mausoleum or shrine of a vicegerent of God for blessing is not an act of blasphemy, but rather an act of respect, admiration, obedience, and seeking nearness to God.

It is ironic that some believe in the virtue of touching the Black Stone, but consider it a sin to touch the grave of Prophet Muhammad!

---

[17] Qur'an, Surah al-Baqarah (2), verse 125.

لَا تَسْجُدُوا لِلشَّمْسِ وَلَا لِلْقَمَرِ وَاسْجُدُوا لِلَّهِ الَّذِي خَلَقَهُنَّ إِن كُنتُمْ إِيَّاهُ تَعْبُدُونَ

> Do not prostrate to the sun, nor to the moon. Prostrate to God, Who created them, if it is He Whom you worship.[18]

According to Islamic scholars, there is a distinction between bowing or prostrating in front of someone or an object while holding belief in the divinity of the said person or thing (which is an act of blasphemy), or not holding this belief. They argue that while prostrating oneself before a person or an object, even if one does not believe in the divinity of that person or object, this is not a recommended act because it might bring about suspicion for some people, even though it is not considered an act of blasphemy. Therefore, since prostration is a symbol of worship, it should only be dedicated to God, and no one or nothing else.

It should be noted that every act of blasphemy is considered to be prohibited, but not every prohibited act is necessarily considered to be an act of blasphemy.

وَأَنَّ الْمَسَاجِدَ لِلَّهِ فَلَا تَدْعُوا مَعَ اللَّهِ أَحَدًا

> And the places of worship are for God; so do not call upon another alongside God.[19]

There is a lot of discussion among scholars concerning the true meaning of the above verse. One group of scholars interpret this verse as the Qur'an stating that the act of prostration in front of a person or thing is a prohibited act, and that it is something

---

[18] Qur'an, Surah Fussilat (41), verse 37.

[19] Qur'an, Surah al-Jinn (72), verse 18.

which is only dedicated for God and should not be performed in front of anyone or anything else.

Another group of scholars put forth the argument that the verse is not stating that prostrating in front of a person or thing is an act of prohibition, but rather prostrating in front of a person or thing becomes a prohibited action if it is done with the intention of believing in the divinity of the said person or thing. They interpret this verse as the Qur'an stating that if one worships God, then they should prostrate before Him, but if one prostrates before a person or thing without believing in their divinity, then it is not considered an act of blasphemy, nor is it a prohibited act.

However, both groups of scholars agree that to prostrate oneself before a person or thing, regardless of the belief in their divinity or not, is not recommended and better to avoid. To bow one's head as a sign of respect to others is acceptable, but to prostrate to anything else is not. The majority of scholars in the School of *Ahlulbayt* believe that to prostrate oneself before anyone or anything other than God is to be avoided.

ما ينبغي لبشر أن يسجد لبشر

> It is not befitting for a human being to prostrate to another human being.

Some might question this belief and give the example of the previously mentioned prostration of Prophet Jacob before Prophet Joseph, but it should be noted that such an act was permissible at that time. With the arrival of Islam, any such act of prostration towards any person or thing became discouraged.

Scholars go one step further in asserting that a believer's worshipping gestures should be absolutely and completely dedicated to God only. Thus, they suggest it is recommended that when someone is praying in a room which has a statue or a portrait of someone, that statue or portrait should be covered or removed so that one's focus is solely dedicated to God.

The Difference between Acts of Worship and Obedience

Islamic scholars further distinguish between acts of worship and acts of obedience: not every act of obedience is considered an act of worship. Some actions are considered to be worship, while others are merely acts of obedience that bring us closer to God. Prayer, fasting, alms giving, etc., are acts of worship (*ibaadah*). They should only be dedicated to God with the intention of seeking nearness to Him. Every act of worship requires the intention of dedication to God (either by one's mouth or heart). Other actions, such as helping a blind person cross the road, feeding the poor, or being dutiful and respectful towards one's parents are acts of obedience (*taa'ah*) and are immensely rewarded by God.

Visiting Holy Shrines

Visiting the shrines of the Prophet and his Household is popular among the Muslim community, especially the followers of the *Ahlulbayt*. There are numerous traditions by the Prophet and Imams which emphasize the great virtue and reward of such visitations (*ziyaarah*).

It is reported that the Prophet said:

من حج بيت ربي ولم يزرني فقد جفاني

> Whoever performs the pilgrimage (to Mecca) and does not visit [my grave in Medina] has done a disservice to me.[20]

[20] *Bihaar al-Anwaar*, Al-Majlisi, vol. 96, pg. 373.

من أتاني زائرا كنت شفيعه يوم القيامة

> Whoever comes to visit me [my grave in Medina], I will be their intercessor on the Day of Judgment.[21]

The least one can say about such visits to the holy shrines is that it is a clear example of revering the symbols of God.

وَمَن يُعَظِّمْ شَعَـٰٓئِرَ ٱللَّهِ فَإِنَّهَا مِن تَقْوَى ٱلْقُلُوبِ

> And whosoever magnifies the symbols of God, truly that comes from the reverence of the hearts.[22]

It is also a major source of inspiration and spiritual empowerment and refinement. The permissibility of building such sacred shrines is also mentioned in the Holy Qur'an.

لَنَتَّخِذَنَّ عَلَيْهِم مَّسْجِدًا

> "Surely we shall build a place of worship over [their graves]."[23]

Some Muslims may raise the question why the followers of the *Ahlulbayt* take an extraordinary interest in visiting the shrine of Imam Hussain in Karbala, Iraq. Visiting the shrine of Imam Hussain is considered to be one of the most important acts of spiritual refinement, and therefore an act of seeking nearness to God. Visitors who flock to the shrine of Imam Hussain do not do so with the intention of worshipping him beside God, rather they go with the intention of paying tribute to an Imam who sacrificed his life and the lives of his family and companions for the sake of God, and to save the religion of Islam. In addition, visitors go to the shrine to demonstrate their love and loyalty for the Prophet

---

[21] *Bihaar al-Anwaar*, vol. 97, pg. 142.
[22] Qur'an, Surah al-Hajj (22), verse 32.
[23] Qur'an, Surah al-Kahf (18), verse 21.

and his family. Imam Hussain stood for universal justice, thus he became an iconic example for all freedom fighters and justice seekers around the world to take lessons from and follow. Millions of souls aspire to march towards his grave and salute him every year. Visiting Imam Hussain's shrine with the intention to seek his intercession is an absolute act of monotheism.

Imam al-Sadiq states:

من أراد الله به الخير قذف في قلبه حب الحسين عليه السلام وحب زيارته ومن أراد الله به السوء قذف في قلبه بغض الحسين وبغض زيارته.

> If God intends goodness for His servant, then He will cast into their heart the love of Hussain and the love of visiting him (his grave); and if God intends evil for someone, then He will cast into their heart the hatred of Hussain and the hatred of his visitation.[24]

Do not Call Apart from God

There are verses in the Qur'an which warn the polytheists about worshiping anything or anyone else besides God. How do we understand them?

وَلَا تَدْعُ مِن دُونِ اللَّهِ مَا لَا يَنفَعُكَ وَلَا يَضُرُّكَ فَإِن فَعَلْتَ فَإِنَّكَ إِذًا مِّنَ الظَّالِمِينَ

> And do not call upon, apart from God, that which neither benefits you, nor harms you. For if you do so, then surely you will be among the wrongdoers.[25]

---

[24] *Jami' Ahadith al-Shi'a*, Burujerdi, vol. 12, pg. 384.
[25] Qur'an, Surah Yunus (10), verse 106.

وَالَّذِينَ تَدْعُونَ مِن دُونِهِ لَا يَسْتَطِيعُونَ نَصْرَكُمْ وَلَا أَنفُسَهُمْ يَنصُرُون

> And those whom you call upon apart from Him can neither help you, nor can they help themselves.[26]

وَالَّذِينَ تَدْعُونَ مِن دُونِهِ مَا يَمْلِكُونَ مِن قِطْمِير

> And as for those upon whom you call apart from Him, they do not possess so much as the husk of a date seed.[27]

If one looks closely, then one will realize that all these verses speak about calling upon idols without God's permission (*Min dunillah*). Calling upon individuals and objects besides God with the belief in their divinity and without the permission of God is an act of apostasy, but calling upon the Prophet and the Imams with the belief in their status as the servants of God and with His permission (*Bi idhnillah*) is an act of monotheism. These two terms will be discussed further in chapter 8.

---

[26] Qur'an, Surah al-A'raaf (7), verse 197.
[27] Qur'an, Surah Faatir (35), verse 13.

7

The Unity and Integrity of God's Guardianship (*Tawheed al-Wilaayah*)

ٱللَّهُ وَلِيُّ ٱلَّذِينَ ءَامَنُوا۟ يُخْرِجُهُم مِّنَ ٱلظُّلُمَـٰتِ إِلَى ٱلنُّورِ

> God is the Protector of those who believe. He brings them out of the darkness into the light.[1]

[1] Qur'an, Surah al-Baqarah (2), verse 257.

The fifth branch of monotheism is *Tawheed al-Wilaayah*, the Unity and Integrity of the Guardianship of God. This concept stresses that God is the Absolute Sovereign in the entire universe. He is in charge of all affairs. This branch can be divided into the Legislative Guardianship (*al-Wilaayah al-Tashri'yyah*) and the Administrative Guardianship (*al-Wilaayah al-Takwiniyyah*). Both branches are under the Supervision and Sovereignty of God.

The Guardianship of Legislation (*al-Wilaayah al-Tashri'yyah*)

The Guardianship of Legislation regulates the life of all creation and has three sub-branches:

1. The right of ruling and judgment (*al-haakimiyyah*): God is the only entity who has the right to rule and judge, as He mentions in the Qur'an:

إِنِ ٱلْحُكْمُ إِلَّا لِلَّهِ

> Judgment belongs to none except God alone.[1]

If the right to rule solely belongs to God, then one might ask about the legitimacy of the rule of others, be it religious leaders or secular ones. According to scholars, if such leaders have been legally and democratically elected by their people, then their rulings are Islamically legitimate. Such rulers should keep in mind that they have been entrusted by their people to uphold justice. Although such a type of government may not necessarily be Islamic, it could be compatible with moral values and people's aspirations.

2. The right of obedience (*al-itaa'ah*): God is the only entity who has the right to be obeyed. Obedience to God is

---

[1] Qur'an, Surah Yusuf (12), verse 40.

achieved through obeying His chosen Apostle and the righteous Imams, who have been referred to in the Qur'an as "those in authority among you:"

يَٰٓأَيُّهَا ٱلَّذِينَ ءَامَنُوٓاْ أَطِيعُواْ ٱللَّهَ وَأَطِيعُواْ ٱلرَّسُولَ وَأُوْلِي ٱلۡأَمۡرِ مِنكُمۡ

> O you who believe! Obey God and obey the Messenger and those in authority among you.[2]

مَّن يُطِعِ ٱلرَّسُولَ فَقَدۡ أَطَاعَ ٱللَّهَ

> Whosoever obeys the Messenger obeys God.[3]

One might ask, what then of God's right of obedience contradicts with obedience towards a leader of a society, be it Islamic or secular? The general answer to this question is that no obedience should be given to any person if it means disobedience to God. However, if a human ruling does not conflict with that of God's rulings, then it would be acceptable to obey it. A person can be in complete obedience towards God and still be a good and law-abiding citizen. Islam stresses upon the importance of the participation of people in the affairs of their societies. If one does not agree with the unethical policies of the country that one resides in, then the solution to this is not an isolation or withdrawal from public life. Fighting corruption and dictatorship necessitates political activism and engagement in the political process to achieve reforms.

3. The right of law-making: God is the only entity who has the right to legislate, because He is the only One who is always Omniscient, Wise, and Just. He neither discriminates against

---

[2] Qur'an, Surah al-Nisaa (4), verse 59.
[3] Qur'an, Surah al-Nisaa (4), verse 80.

people, nor does He exercise oppression, nepotism, or favoritism. Furthermore, God states:

يقول الله تعالى: يا بن آدم، لم أخلقك لأربح عليك، إنما خلقتك لتربح على

> "O son of Adam! God did not create mankind to be of benefit to Him, but for mankind to benefit from Him."[4]

The Guardianship of Administration of the Universe (*al-Wilaayah al-Takwiniyyah*)

The second branch of the Unity of God's Guardianship is the Integrity of God in matters of the creation and administration of the universe (*al-Wilaayah al-Takwiniyyah*). Under this concept, two important Qur'anic terms, *al-Mudabiriyyah* and *al-Rububiyyah*, are studied. The following Qur'anic verses refer to this concept:

وَخَلَقَ كُلَّ شَيْءٍ فَقَدَّرَهُۥ تَقْدِيرًا

> And Who created everything, then measured it out with due measure.[5]

سَبِّحِ ٱسْمَ رَبِّكَ ٱلْأَعْلَى ٱلَّذِى خَلَقَ فَسَوَّىٰ وَٱلَّذِى قَدَّرَ فَهَدَىٰ

> Glorify the name of your Lord, the Most High, Who created then fashioned, Who measured out then guided.[6]

قَالَ فَمَن رَّبُّكُمَا يَـٰمُوسَىٰ

> [Pharaoh] said: "So who is the Lord of you two, O Moses?"[7]

---

[4] *Sharh Nahj al-Balagha*, Ibn Abi al-Hadid, vol. 20, pg. 319.
[5] Qur'an, Surah al-Furqaan (25), verse 2.
[6] Qur'an, Surah al-A'laa (87), verses 1-3.
[7] Qur'an, Surah Taha (20), verse 49.

قَالَ رَبُّنَا ٱلَّذِىٓ أَعْطَىٰ كُلَّ شَىْءٍ خَلْقَهُۥ ثُمَّ هَدَىٰ

> He said: "Our Lord is He Who gives everything its creation, then guides [it]."[8]

If we analyze the descriptions of God in the Qur'an, we will notice that the Qur'an lays special emphasis on the word "*Al-Rabb*" which is derived from the word "*Tarbiyyah,*" meaning 'to follow up on something,' and the word "*Rububiyyah,*" meaning 'cherishing and sustaining.' The concept of "*Tarbiyyah,*" as it relates to God, is very important in monotheism, because God is not only the Creator, but He is also the Cherisher and the Sustainer.

God is Omnipresent, and is always attentive when it comes to all of His creation. He is All-Hearing and All-Seeing. Therefore, the Qur'an emphasizes on God's role, not only as a Creator, but also as the One who tends to the needs of His creations in this life. On the Day of Judgment, unlike the courts on Earth that often take a long time to process cases, God will not grow tired of tending to the fate of billions of people in a matter of no time.

إِنَّا كُلَّ شَىْءٍ خَلَقْنَٰهُ بِقَدَرٍ ۝ وَمَآ أَمْرُنَآ إِلَّا وَٰحِدَةٌ كَلَمْحٍۭ بِٱلْبَصَرِ

> Truly We created everything according to a measure. And Our Command is naught but one, like the blinking of an eye.[9]

During the pre-Islamic times in the Arabian Peninsula, some of the pagans accepted God as the Creator, but not as the Legislator.

---

[8] Qur'an, Surah Taha (20), verse 50.
[9] Qur'an, Surah al-Qamar (54), verses 49-50.

وَلَئِن سَأَلْتَهُم مَّنْ خَلَقَ ٱلسَّمَٰوَٰتِ وَٱلْأَرْضَ وَسَخَّرَ ٱلشَّمْسَ
وَٱلْقَمَرَ لَيَقُولُنَّ ٱللَّهُ ۖ فَأَنَّىٰ يُؤْفَكُونَ

> If you were to ask them: "Who created the heavens and the earth, and made the sun and the moon subservient?" They would surely say: "God." How then, are they deluded?[10]

The type of polytheism which existed in the Arabian Peninsula was the belief that although God was the Creator, He was not an Administrator. They worshipped other objects, because they believed that God could not administer the entire universe's affairs on His own, so instead He gave that responsibility to the celestial objects. Their disbelief in the Unity and Integrity of God stemmed from their belief that He was not in charge.

God's Characteristics as the Provider and Nurturer negate such a belief. Before the pagan Arabs, the people of Prophet Abraham in Mesopotamia subscribed to this incomplete notion of God as well. Although they believed in God as a Creator, they worshipped the sun and the moon as the administrators of the affairs of the universe. Thus, Prophet Abraham decided to challenge his people's views on lordship. The Qur'an beautifully depicts how he did this as follows:

فَلَمَّا رَءَا ٱلشَّمْسَ بَازِغَةً قَالَ هَٰذَا رَبِّى هَٰذَآ أَكْبَرُ ۖ فَلَمَّآ أَفَلَتْ
قَالَ يَٰقَوْمِ إِنِّى بَرِىٓءٌ مِّمَّا تُشْرِكُونَ

> Then when he saw the sun rising, he said: "This is my Lord! This is greater!" But when it set, he said: "O my people! Truly I reject whatever you associate with God.[11]

---

[10] Qur'an, Surah al-Ankaboot (29), verse 61.
[11] Qur'an, Surah al-An'aam (6), verse 78.

Prophet Abraham warned his people that they were worshiping the wrong objects. He explained to them that the object of their worship, which was only available during the day for a short period of time, cannot possibly be in charge of the affairs of the universe; thus he advised them to turn to the One True God by saying the following words:

إِنِّي وَجَّهْتُ وَجْهِيَ لِلَّذِي فَطَرَ ٱلسَّمَٰوَٰتِ وَٱلْأَرْضَ حَنِيفًاۖ وَمَآ أَنَا۠ مِنَ ٱلْمُشْرِكِينَ

> Truly, as a *hanif* (upright one following pure monotheism), I have turned my face towards Him Who created the heavens and the earth, and I am not of the idolaters."[12]

The reason why God is in charge, and not something or someone else, is because it is only Him who enjoys unique Attributes such as being Self-Subsisting, All-Aware, Ever-Present, and Tentative at all times.

Abraham and his son, Ishmael, introduced monotheism to the Arabs of Mecca. However, as time passed, people began to drift away from pure monotheism and began to worship idols, as described earlier in this book. It seems that polytheism crept into Mecca through an Arab merchant who had traveled to Syria. He brought an idol by the name of Hubal and placed it on the top of the Ka'bah, and asked people to worship it. Gradually, the people of Mecca began to call upon Hubal for help, thinking that it was in charge of the affairs of the universe. During the Battle of Badr against the Prophet of Islam, the Meccans called upon Hubal for victory against the Muslims.

The same notion of seeking help from idols existed with earlier communities as well. It is believed that between the time

---

[12] Qur'an, Surah al-An'aam (6), verse 79.

of Prophet Adam and Prophet Noah, there were five pious people by the name of Wadd, Suwaa', Yaghuth, Ya'ooq, and Nasr. When they died, people erected statues of them and started to worship them. Their names are mentioned in the Qur'an:

وَمَكَرُواْ مَكۡرٗا كُبَّارٗا ۝ وَقَالُواْ لَا تَذَرُنَّ ءَالِهَتَكُمۡ وَلَا تَذَرُنَّ وَدّٗا وَلَا سُوَاعٗا وَلَا يَغُوثَ وَيَعُوقَ وَنَسۡرٗا

> And they devised a mighty plot, saying, "Do not leave your gods; do not leave Wadd or Suwaa'; or Yaghuth; Ya'ooq; or Nasr."[13]

People petitioned them for help and provision.

مَا نَعۡبُدُهُمۡ إِلَّا لِيُقَرِّبُونَآ إِلَى ٱللَّهِ زُلۡفَىٰٓ

> "We do not worship them except so that they may bring us nearer to God."[14]

It might come across the mind of the reader that Muslims too, when calling upon the Prophet or the Imams for help, may emulate the practices of the polytheists in calling upon their idols for help. However, unlike the idolaters, who believed in the divinity and independence of their idols, Muslims who seek help and guidance from the Prophet and Imams do not believe in their divinity, nor do they believe that they are independent entities from God. The upcoming chapter will delve into this topic in further detail.

---

[13] Qur'an, Surah Nuh (71), verses 22-23.
[14] Qur'an, Surah al-Zumar (39), verse 3.

The Integrity of the Administration of the Universe (*Tawheed al-Mudabiriyyah*)

One of the descriptions of God in the Qur'an is the Administrator of the universe (*Al-Mudabbir*). God does not only create, but He administers all of the affairs as well.

ٱللَّهُ ٱلَّذِى رَفَعَ ٱلسَّمَٰوَٰتِ بِغَيْرِ عَمَدٍ تَرَوْنَهَا ۖ ثُمَّ ٱسْتَوَىٰ عَلَى
ٱلْعَرْشِ ۖ وَسَخَّرَ ٱلشَّمْسَ وَٱلْقَمَرَ ۖ كُلٌّ يَجْرِى لِأَجَلٍ مُّسَمًّى ۚ يُدَبِّرُ
ٱلْأَمْرَ يُفَصِّلُ ٱلْءَايَٰتِ لَعَلَّكُم بِلِقَآءِ رَبِّكُمْ تُوقِنُونَ

> God it is Who raised the heavens without pillars that you see, then established Himself above the Throne; and He made the sun and the moon subservient, each running for a term appointed. He directs the affair, expounds the signs, so that you may be certain of the meeting with your Lord.[15]

As the Guardian of the Administration of the universe, God is the Creator, Sustainer, Nurturer, and, most importantly, the Administrator of everything in existence.

مَا مِن شَفِيعٍ إِلَّا مِنۢ بَعْدِ إِذْنِهِۦ

> There is no intercessor except by His permission.[16]

Nothing can intercede for anything else in this universe except with His permission. In this particular verse, "*shafa'a*" does not refer to the intercession in the hereafter, rather it is the intercession of the administration and management of this universe. In other words, it means that God does not need any aid in managing the affairs of this universe. He is the only source of power for everything which exists.

---

[15] Qur'an, Surah al-Ra'd (13), verse 2.
[16] Qur'an, Surah Yunus (10), verse 3.

As discussed earlier, everything in this universe is based on the principle of cause and effect. God is the cause of every action in the universe. He created the means to produce an effect from every natural force. Likewise, His vicegerents and scriptures are means that He sent down to invite His creations towards His one True Path. None of these means would be able to create any effect without God's permission.

تأثير اية علة في هذا الكون منوط بالإذن الإلهي

> The effect of any cause in this universe depends completely on God's permission.

When the Qur'an describes God, it lays emphasis on God as the Administrator as well.

أَلَا لَهُ ٱلْخَلْقُ وَٱلْأَمْرُ

> Truly to Him belongs the creation and the command.[17]

It is erroneous to assume that God is only the Creator and not the Administrator, or vice versa. In chapter 55 of the Qur'an, Surah al-Rahmaan, the following verse has been repeated thirty-one times:

فَبِأَيِّ ءَالَآءِ رَبِّكُمَا تُكَذِّبَانِ

> So which of the favors of your Lord will you deny?

This verse has been mentioned with this frequency, because one can only grasp the idea through such repetition. This verse reiterates God's role as the Administrator of the affairs of the entire universe.

[17] Qur'an, Surah al-A'raaf (7), verse 54.

8

Intercession and Monotheism

قُل لِّلَّهِ الشَّفَاعَةُ جَمِيعًا

> Say: "To God belongs (the right to) intercession entirely."[1]

[1] Qur'an, Surah al-Zumar (39), verse 44.

One of the most widely debated topics related to the principle of monotheism is the concept of intercession (*shafa'ah*).

مَن ذَا ٱلَّذِى يَشْفَعُ عِندَهُۥٓ إِلَّا بِإِذْنِهِ

> Who is there that may intercede with Him except by His permission?[1]

Some schools of thought in Islam refute the concept of intercession altogether and consider it to be unacceptable; whereas other schools of thought embrace this Qur'anic concept. This debate is generated because of two types of verses in the Qur'an regarding intercession.

One set of verses states that intercession is a right which belongs only to God.

قُل لِّلَّهِ الشَّفَاعَةُ جَمِيعًا

> Say: "To God belongs (the right to) intercession entirely."[2]

The other set of verses asserts that although the right of intercession belongs only to Him, He may bestow it on whomsoever He pleases.

وَكَم مِّن مَّلَكٍ فِي السَّمَاوَاتِ لَا تُغْنِي شَفَاعَتُهُمْ شَيْئًا إِلَّا مِن
بَعْدِ أَن يَأْذَنَ اللَّهُ لِمَن يَشَاءُ وَيَرْضَى

> And how many an angel is there in the heavens whose intercession will not avail except after God grants permission to whomsoever He wills and unto the one with whom He is content.[3]

---

[1] Qur'an, Surah al-Baqarah (2), verse 255.
[2] Qur'an, Surah al-Zumar (39), verse 44.
[3] Qur'an, Surah al-Najm (53), verse 26.

One must note that the Qur'an uses two important terms in relation to seeking help from God. One term is *Bi idhnillah,* and the other term is *Min dunillah.*

Bi idhnillah means 'seeking help (from others) with God's permission' which is entirely lawful. Calling upon Prophet Muhammad and his progeny is with God's permission and authorization, since they do not act independently from Him, rather, they are His agents, representing the path to Him. The two aforementioned types of verses do not contradict one another, for when one calls upon the Prophet and his progeny, one is in fact calling upon God.

Seeking help from others without God's permission is considered an act of apostasy or heresy, and is not permissible. This is what the Qur'an refers to as *Min dunillah.* It is seeking spiritual guidance or intercession from an idol or a person without God's permission, and with the belief that this idol or person acts independently from God.

God can choose whomsoever He wills, and elevate them to a worthy position so that they can intercede on behalf of their community with God's permission, as it is illustrated in the Qur'an:

عَسَىٰٓ أَن يَبْعَثَكَ رَبُّكَ مَقَامًا مَّحْمُودًا

> It may be that your Lord will resurrect you to a praiseworthy station.[4]

The term "praiseworthy station (*maqaam al-mahmood*)" has been interpreted by the Imams of the *Ahlulbayt* as the 'position of intercession.' Imam Ali states that the above verse is the most promising one in the Qur'an, since it gifts the Prophet with the power of intercession. Some Sunni sources (*Fathul Qadir,*

[4] Qur'an, Surah al-Isra (17), verse 79.

Shawkaani, vol. 3, pg. 316; and *Tareekh Baghdad*, Al-Khatib, vol. 8, pg. 52; and others) explain this "praiseworthy station" as the Prophet sitting next to God on His Throne on the Day of Judgment!

Furthermore, God in the Qur'an correlates obedience to Him with obedience to the Prophet (see Qur'an 4:80), as well as with obedience to those who are in charge (see Qur'an 4:59). On the other hand, God correlates disobedience to Him with disobedience to the Prophet (see Qur'an 4:14).

Moreover, in some instances in the Qur'an, God conditions seeking His forgiveness through the intercession of the Prophet.

وَمَآ أَرۡسَلۡنَا مِن رَّسُولٍ إِلَّا لِيُطَاعَ بِإِذۡنِ ٱللَّهِۚ وَلَوۡ أَنَّهُمۡ إِذ ظَّلَمُوٓاْ أَنفُسَهُمۡ جَآءُوكَ فَٱسۡتَغۡفَرُواْ ٱللَّهَ وَٱسۡتَغۡفَرَ لَهُمُ ٱلرَّسُولُ لَوَجَدُواْ ٱللَّهَ تَوَّابًا رَّحِيمًا

> And We sent no messenger except that he should be obeyed by God's permission. And if, when they had wronged themselves, they had but come to you (O Muhammad) and asked forgiveness of God, and the Messenger had asked forgiveness for them, they would surely have found God Oft-Forgiving, All-Merciful.[5]

This verse describes Prophet Muhammad seeking repentance and forgiveness on behalf of some members of his community, as an act of pure faith. This is a clear invitation from God to the believers to call upon the Prophet for intercession.

The Qur'an encourages believers to seek intercession, and states that those who do not seek the Prophet's intercession are hypocrites.

---

[5] Qur'an, Surah al-Nisaa (4), verse 64.

وَإِذَا قِيلَ لَهُمْ تَعَالَوْا۟ يَسْتَغْفِرْ لَكُمْ رَسُولُ ٱللَّهِ لَوَّوْا۟ رُءُوسَهُمْ
وَرَأَيْتَهُمْ يَصُدُّونَ وَهُم مُّسْتَكْبِرُونَ

> And when it is said unto them: "Come! The Messenger of God will ask forgiveness for you," they twist their heads, and you see them turning away in arrogance.[6]

This verse narrates the story of those sinners who rejected the idea of the Prophet interceding for them. However, one must understand the fact that to ask the Prophet for intercession is not an act which invalidates one's faith, but rather it is one that enhances one's faith.

There are narrations in Sunni traditions, as well as in Shi'a ones, which state that when people experienced drought and famine, Prophet Muhammad's companions would come to him and ask him to pray for their relief from the disaster. They realized that their prayers alone might not be answered by God, unless they are accompanied by the prayers of the Prophet.

Anas ibn Malik, a companion of the Prophet, narrates that one day he went to the Prophet and asked for his intercession because of the drought that was severely hurting the people. The Prophet raised his hands up to pray, and when he put his hands down, the sky was covered with clouds and it started to rain. It rained continuously from one Friday to another, because the Prophet interceded for the community.

During the time of Prophet Jesus, people came to him and asked him to cure their illnesses, as an act of faith.

---

[6] Qur'an, Surah al-Munafiqoon (63), verse 5.

وَأُبْرِئُ ٱلْأَكْمَهَ وَٱلْأَبْرَصَ وَأُحْيِ ٱلْمَوْتَىٰ بِإِذْنِ ٱللَّهِ

> "And I [Jesus] will heal the blind, and the leper, and give life to the dead by God's permission."[7]

People approached Jesus believing that he was sent by God and worked for God. In this regard, he interceded on behalf of God, and with God's permission, in order to heal the blind and the ill.

Another example of intercession of the Prophets from the Qur'an is the story of the sons of Prophet Jacob. When the plot to kill their brother Joseph came to light forty years later, they begged their father to seek God's forgiveness for them:

قَالُوا۟ يَٰٓأَبَانَا ٱسْتَغْفِرْ لَنَا ذُنُوبَنَآ إِنَّا كُنَّا خَٰطِـِٔينَ

> They said: "O father! Seek forgiveness for us for our sins. Truly we were at fault."[8]

If interceding for someone was an act of blasphemy, then Jacob, a Messenger sent by God, would have deterred his sons from seeking his intercession (for similar stories see Qur'an 4:64 and 12:93, further elaborated on in Chapter 10).

A story similar to this is that of Prophet Moses and the children of Israel in the Sinai Peninsula. When they were in the Sinai Peninsula, they did not have any drinking water. The Israelites asked Prophet Moses to intercede for them and ask God to send them drinking water. The Israelites asking for the intercession of Moses at a time of need was not an act of blasphemy either, rather it was an act of monotheism.

---

[7] Qur'an, Surah Ale Imraan (3), verse 49.
[8] Qur'an, Surah Yusuf (12), verse 97.

وَإِذِ ٱسۡتَسۡقَىٰ مُوسَىٰ لِقَوۡمِهِۦ فَقُلۡنَا ٱضۡرِب بِّعَصَاكَ ٱلۡحَجَرَۖ
فَٱنفَجَرَتۡ مِنۡهُ ٱثۡنَتَا عَشۡرَةَ عَيۡنٗاۖ قَدۡ عَلِمَ كُلُّ أُنَاسٖ مَّشۡرَبَهُمۡۖ
كُلُواْ وَٱشۡرَبُواْ مِن رِّزۡقِ ٱللَّهِ وَلَا تَعۡثَوۡاْ فِي ٱلۡأَرۡضِ مُفۡسِدِينَ

> And when Moses prayed for water for his people, We said: "Strike the rock with your staff." Then twelve springs gushed forth from it; and each people (tribe) knew their drinking place. "Eat and drink from the provision of God, and behave not wickedly upon the earth, spreading corruption."[9]

They realized that the only reason why Moses could help them was because God had given him the ability and permission to perform a miracle.

Going back to the time of Prophet Muhammad, there are authentic narrations which state that when the Prophet would perform ablution, his companions would gather around him to collect the water which was flowing down from his face and arms, then they would pour that water on their faces for blessing. It would get so crowded, that the companions would fight with one another to get access to the remnants of the water that he used.[10] In the books of Sahih, such as Bukhari and Muslim, there are chapters which are dedicated to describing how the Muslims sought blessings from the food and drink of the Prophet as well.[11] It has also been narrated that at times, they would take care to not allow the hair of the Prophet to reach the ground, as even his hair was treated as a blessing.[12]

---

9 Qur'an, Surah al-Baqarah (2), verse 60.

10 *Fath al-Bari – The Commentary on Sahih Bukhari*, Chapter on Wudhu, vol. 1, pg. 354, trad. #189.

11 Ibid., vol. 1, pg. 353, trad. #187.

12 Ibid., vol. 1, pg. 295 and pg. 353.

When Medina faced a famine during Umar's caliphate, Umar went to the uncle of the Prophet, Al-Abbas, and asked him to intercede so that the famine would end. Al-Abbas was initially a non-believer who fought against the Prophet in the battle of Badr, but he accepted Islam in Medina after this battle.

Another narration states that Hudhaifah ibn al-Yamani, one of the companions of the Prophet, came to the Prophet one day to ask him to intercede and seek forgiveness for his mother and him. Prophet Muhammad assured him that he will pray for his mother and him, and that God will forgive them.

Once the Prophet would finish his afternoon prayers, the people of Medina would bring him dishes containing water, and he would put his hands into the water to bless it. They would then take these dishes back to their families and use the water as blessed water. If this was an act of blasphemy, then the Prophet would have never partaken in blessing the water (for further references, see Fath al-Bari/Bukhari 7/643, #4328; and Sahih Muslim, Book of Drinks, 3/1604 #2030, 3/1623 #2053). Imam Bukhari's book mentions that after the death of the Prophet, Muslims would seek blessings from his personal belongings, such as his sword, cane, dish, ring, hair, and sandals.

God Assigns Responsibilities

Part of the belief in the Unity and Integrity of Guardianship (*Tawheed al-Wilaayah*), as discussed in the previous chapter, is the belief that God is responsible for the management of the entire universe. *Tawheed al-Mudabbariyyah* is the belief that every action in this universe falls under God's control and supervision.

Earlier in this book, it was discussed that angels exist and perform certain tasks, while all power of the universe belongs solely to God. We elaborated on the question whether this undermines His Power or not, and concluded that this is not the case as angels do not work independently from God. God is the only Sovereign Power in this universe and angels strictly obey Him. He commissions angels as managers and protectors. If angels or others work independently from God, then this would undermine His Sovereignty.

فَالْمُدَبِّرَاتِ أَمْرً

> By those [angels] who govern affairs.[13]

Tadbir means "to arrange." In this verse, "those'' refers to the angels who manage this world's affairs with God's permission. They do not work independently from God, but they work for God. Another verse in the Qur'an refers to the role of the angels:

وَهُوَ الْقَاهِرُ فَوْقَ عِبَادِهِ وَيُرْسِلُ عَلَيْكُمْ حَفَظَةً

> And He is Dominant over His servants. He sends guardians (angels) over you.[14]

One has to understand that the Unity of Deeds does not necessarily entail that God should execute everything by Himself. It means that no action takes place in this universe without the permission of God. If He wishes, He can bestow some of the responsibilities to the angels or others, even though He is not in need of any help. God decreed that this universe should be governed by the principle of cause and effect. This is a lesson for humanity on the importance of collective work.

---

[13] Qur'an, Surah al-Nazi'aat (79), verse 5.
[14] Qur'an, Surah al-An'aam (6), verse 61.

إِنَّمَا أَمْرُهُ إِذَا أَرَادَ شَيْئًا أَن يَقُولَ لَهُ كُن فَيَكُونَ

> His Command when He desires a thing is only to say to it: "Be!" and it is.[15]

God can do whatever He wishes in no time at all, it does not even take a fraction of a second. By bestowing the angels with certain responsibilities, God teaches us that life is based on assigning tasks to others, and there is a precise system of discipline and responsibilities which must take place on earth.

The following verses from the Qur'an are examples of how God assigns tasks for angels, Prophets, and other agents to administer the affairs of the universe.

لَّا يَعْصُونَ اللَّهَ مَا أَمَرَهُمْ وَيَفْعَلُونَ مَا يُؤْمَرُونَ

> They [the angels] do not disobey God in what He commands of them, and they do whatever they are commanded.[16]

In the above verse, angels have been described as being servants of God and not having free will.

Although all souls belong to God, and it is God who is responsible for death, it is the Angel of Death who has been given the authority to receive the souls. This angel does not get to pick and choose whose soul to take, as he is completely instructed by God.

اللَّهُ يَتَوَفَّى الْأَنفُسَ حِينَ مَوْتِهَا

> God takes the souls at the moment of their death.[17]

---

[15] Qur'an, Surah Yaseen (36), verse 82.
[16] Qur'an, Surah al-Tahreem (66), verse 6.
[17] Qur'an, Surah al-Zumar (39), verse 42.

قُلْ يَتَوَفَّاكُم مَّلَكُ الْمَوْتِ الَّذِى وُكِّلَ بِكُ

> Say: "The Angel of Death who has been entrusted with you, will take you."[18]

حَتَّىٰٓ إِذَا جَاءَ أَحَدَكُمُ الْمَوْتُ تَوَفَّتْهُ رُسُلُنَا

> When death comes to one of you, Our messengers (angels) will take them.[19]

In conclusion, God's Sovereignty and Authority is not compromised by instructing angels to carry out certain responsibilities.

Knowledge of the Unseen (*'Ilmul Ghaib*)

Another topic which is equally debated among the various schools of thought is the "Knowledge of the Unseen" (*'Ilmul Ghaib*). All knowledge belongs to God, seen or Unseen. Like intercession, God gives Knowledge of the Unseen to whomsoever He chooses and to the extent that He chooses. The Qur'an asserts:

قُل لَّا يَعْلَمُ مَن فِى السَّمَاوَاتِ وَالْأَرْضِ الْغَيْبَ إِلَّا اللَّهُ

> Say: "None in the heavens or on the earth know the Unseen except God."[20]

عَالِمُ الْغَيْبِ فَلَا يُظْهِرُ عَلَىٰ غَيْبِهِ أَحَدًا

> Knower of the Unseen, He does not disclose His (Knowledge of the) Unseen to anyone.[21]

---

[18] Qur'an, Surah al-Sajdah (32), verse 11.
[19] Qur'an, Surah al-An'aam (6), verse 61.
[20] Qur'an, Surah al-Naml (27), verse 65.
[21] Qur'an, Surah al-Jinn (72), verse 26.

إِلَّا مَنِ ارْتَضَىٰ مِن رَّسُولٍ

> Except to the one whom He approves as a Messenger.[22]

وَمَا كَانَ اللَّهُ لِيُطْلِعَكُمْ عَلَى الْغَيْبِ وَلَٰكِنَّ اللَّهَ يَجْتَبِي مِن رُّسُلِهِ مَن يَشَاءُ

> And God will not apprise you of the Unseen, but God chooses from His messengers whomsoever He will.[23]

These verses are a response to those who question an apostle or messenger's knowledge of the Unseen. Again, it must be clear that by giving this authority to certain figures, God's own Authority and Sovereignty is never compromised. He shares His Knowledge of the Unseen with whomsoever He wills.

---

[22] Qur'an, Surah al-Jinn (72), verse 27.
[23] Qur'an, Surah Ale Imraan (3), verse 179.

9

Relegation *(Al-Tafweedh)*

وَمَآ ءَاتَىٰكُمُ ٱلرَّسُولُ فَخُذُوهُ وَمَا نَهَىٰكُمْ عَنْهُ فَٱنتَهُوا۟

> And whatsoever the Messenger gives you, take it; and whatsoever he forbids you from, forgo that.[1]

[1] Qur'an, Surah al-Hashr (59), verse 7.

In light of continuing the discussion on intercession, this chapter elaborates on the concept of *Al-Tafweedh,* another contentious topic of discussion among the scholars of theology. In this specific context, *Al-Tafweedh* is the belief that God relegates some of His Responsibilities and Powers to certain beings.

Belief in this concept predates Islam. Polytheists in pre-Islamic Arabia used to worship *jinns* and angels because they believed that God had left His position of power and put the *jinns* and angels in charge of the universe. They believed that these beings had the power to direct the course of the universe however they pleased.

وَمِنَ ٱلنَّاسِ مَن يَتَّخِذُ مِن دُونِ ٱللَّهِ أَندَادًا يُحِبُّونَهُمْ كَحُبِّ ٱللَّهِ

> And among the people there are some who take up equals apart from God, loving them like (they should be) loving God.[1]

Such a concept is considered to be a type of disbelief in God and is an absolute declaration of polytheistic belief.

In the Islamic era, there were two main types of *Al-Tafweedh* that emerged among some of the theologians: *Al-Tafweedh al-Takwini,* and *Al-Tafweedh al-Tashriee. Al-Tafweedh al-Takwini* is divided into two parts: the Exclusive (*al-Khaas*) Delegation, and the Inclusive (*al-'Aam*) Delegation. Both of these types are rejected by the mainstream theologians, as we are going to examine.

The Exclusive Relegation (*Al-Tafweedh al-Takwini al-Khaas*)

The exclusive type of *Al-Tafweedh* (*al-Khaas*) states that God has completely delegated the matters of creation, sustenance,

[1] Qur'an, Surah al-Baqarah (2), verse 165.

provision, and death to Prophet Muhammad and the Imams after him. Furthermore, Al-Mufeed, in his work *Awaa'il al-Maqaalat;* and Al-Tusi in his work *Al-Ghaybah,* argue that the followers of this type of *Al-Tafweedh* held the belief that the Imams were divine and did not die, but only appeared to have died to the people. This type of *Al-Tafweedh* is categorically rejected by the Imams of the School of the *Ahlulbayt.* On the following pages, narrations from Imam al-Sadiq and Imam al-Ridha regarding this subject will be discussed. The scholars of Shia Islam, such as Al-Sadooq, Al-Mufeed, and Al-Tusi refute this ideology, and emphasize that it is considered the most radical form of exaggeration (*ghuluw*), which in turn is a form of polytheism (*shirk*). Apparently, the advocates of exclusive *Al-Tafweedh* no longer exist.

The Qur'an stresses that matters of creation, giving life, causing death, and provision are exclusive rights that belong to God alone, and He does not have any helper, nor partner in this regard.

أَلَا لَهُ ٱلْخَلْقُ وَٱلْأَمْرُ

> Do not creation and command belong (solely) to Him?[2]

قُلْ هَلْ مِن شُرَكَآئِكُم مَّن يَبْدَؤُا۟ ٱلْخَلْقَ ثُمَّ يُعِيدُهُۥ ۚ قُلِ ٱللَّهُ
يَبْدَؤُا۟ ٱلْخَلْقَ ثُمَّ يُعِيدُهُۥ ۖ فَأَنَّىٰ تُؤْفَكُونَ

> Say: "Is there among your partners, anyone who originates creation and then brings it back?" Say: "God originates creation, then brings it back. How then, are you deluded?"[3]

Sustenance is the exclusive right of God as well:

---

[2] Qur'an, Surah al-A'raaf (7), verse 54.
[3] Qur'an, Surah Yunus (10), verse 34.

وَمَن يَرْزُقُكُم مِّنَ ٱلسَّمَآءِ وَٱلْأَرْضِ ۗ أَءِلَـٰهٌ مَّعَ ٱللَّهِ

> And who provides for you from the heaven and the earth? Is there a deity alongside God?[4]

It is worth mentioning that the Holy Qur'an quotes the words of Prophet Jesus as follows:

أَنِّىٓ أَخْلُقُ لَكُم مِّنَ ٱلطِّينِ كَهَيْـَٔةِ ٱلطَّيْرِ فَأَنفُخُ فِيهِ فَيَكُونُ طَيْرًۢا بِإِذْنِ ٱللَّهِ

> "I will create for you out of clay the shape of a bird. Then I will breathe into it, and it will be a bird by the permission of God."[5]

This act of "creation by Jesus" was not a case of *Tafweedh al-Khaas.* It was a temporary power given to Prophet Jesus by God to perform miracles for a certain period of time - God did not relegate His complete Power to Jesus permanently, nor did He surrender His Authority to him. Jesus was dependent upon God, and performed miracles on behalf of Him and only with His permission.

Imam al-Ridha has said:

الغلاة كفار والمفوضة مشركون

> The exaggerators (*ghulaat*) are concealers of faith, and those who believe in *Al-Tafweedh* are polytheists.[6]

Imam al-Ridha also said:

---

[4] Qur'an, Surah al-Naml (27), verse 64.
[5] Qur'an, Surah Ale Imraan (3), verse 49.
[6] *'Uyoon Akhbar al-Ridha,* Al-Sadooq, vol. 1, pg. 219.

ومن زعم أن الله عز وجل فوض أمر الخلق والرزق إلى حججه عليهم السلام فقد قال بالتفويض، والقائل بالتفويض مشرك

Whoever alleges that God has transferred His Power pertaining to the affairs of the creatures to His Imams, or believes in *Al-Tafweedh*, or believes in [absolute] *Al-Tafweedh* is a polytheist.[7]

وعن زرارة أنه قال، قلت للصادق عليه السلام: إن رجلا يقول بالتفويض. قال عليه السلام: وما التفويض؟ قلت: يقول: إن الله عز وجل خلق محمدا صلى الله عليه وآله وسلم وعليا عليه السلام ثم فوض الأمر إليهما ، فخلقا، ورزقا، وأحيا، وأماتا. فقال: كذب عدو الله، إذا رجعت إليه فاقرأ عليه الآية التي في سورة الرعد (أم جعلوا لله شركاء خلقوا كخلقه فتشابه الخلق عليهم قل الله خالق كل شئ وهو الواحد القاهر). فانصرفت إلى الرجل فأخبرته بما قال الصادق عليه السلام فكأنما ألقمته حجرا، أو قال: فكأنما خرس

Zurarah ibn A'yun, a companion of Imam al-Sadiq, once told the Imam that he overheard someone claim that he believes in *Al-Tafweedh* (the man believed in *Al-Tafweedh* and said that God created Prophet Muhammad and Imam Ali, and transferred His Power to them so that they had the power to create, sustain, end, and bring forth life). Upon hearing this, the Imam replied: "This opponent of God has lied - recite for him the verse in Surah al-Ra'd which says: "Or have they ascribed unto God partners who created the like of His creation, such that creation seems alike to them?

[7] *Bihaar al-Anwaar*, Allamah al-Majlisi, vol. 25, pg. 329.

> Say: 'God is the Creator of all things, and He is the One, the Paramount.'"[8]

As believers in God's Wisdom, our belief in monotheism should be the way that He has willed and intended for it to be. Excessive love for the Prophets and Imams should not make a person believe that they are divine beings. Imam al-Sadiq warned his followers about fabricated narrations against the *Ahlulbayt* that refer to the Imams as having divine qualities which belong only to God.

يقول المجلسي: وأما التفويض فيطلق على معان بعضها منفي عنهم عليهم السلام وبعضها مثبت لهم، فالأول التفويض في الخلق والرزق والتربية والإماتة والاحياء، فإن قوما قالوا: إن الله تعالى خلقهم وفوض إليهم أمر الخلق فهم يخلقون ويرزقون ويميتون ويحيون، وهذا الكلام يحتمل وجهين:

أحدهما أن يقال: إنهم يفعلون جميع ذلك بقدرتهم وإرادتهم وهم الفاعلون حقيقة، وهذا كفر صريح دلت على استحالته الأدلة العقلية والنقلية، ولا يستريب عاقل في كفر من قال به.

وثانيهما: أن الله تعالى يفعل ذلك مقارنا لإرادتهم كشق القمر وإحياء الموتى وقلب العصا حية وغير ذلك من المعجزات ، فإن جميع ذلك إنما تحصل بقدرته تعالى مقارنا لإرادتهم لظهور صدقهم، فلا يأبى العقل عن أن يكون الله تعالى خلقهم وأكملهم وألهمهم ما يصلح في نظام العالم، ثم خلق كل شئ مقارنا لإرادتهم

[8] Qur'an, Surah al-Ra'd (13), verse 16.

ومشيتهم .وهذا وإن كان العقل لا يعارضه كفاحا لكن الاخبار السالفة تمنع من القول به فيما عدا المعجزات ظاهرا بل صراحا ، مع أن القول به قول بما لا يعلم إذ لم يرد ذلك في الأخبار المعتبرة فيما نعلم

Allamah al-Majlisi, a 12th century transmitter of narrations (*hadith*), explains the concept of *Al-Tafweedh,* and the stance of the School of *Ahlulbayt* regarding it. He argues that part of *Al-Tafweedh* applies, while other parts do not. As for the parts which do not apply to the Prophets and Imams, they are: creation, provision, nourishment, death, and resurrection. If a person believes that the Prophets and Imams practice the aforementioned activities independently from God through their own power and will, then this is a very apparent disbelief; and furthermore, this belief is impossible due to rational and traditional evidence. The other part of *Al-Tafweedh*, which could apply to the Prophets and Imams who are the vicegerents of God, is that God Himself undertakes the affairs of life, death, sustenance, etc., in a manner which supports the objectives of those vicegerents. The above explanation does not conflict with reason; however, it was illustrated only through miracles, and there is no sufficient evidence to prove it other than miracles.

The Inclusive Relegation (*Al-Tafweedh al-Takwini al-'Aam*)

The second form of *Al-Tafweedh al-Takwini* is the general one (*al-'Aam*). This type of *Al-Tafweedh* is advocated by the Mu'tazilites, who argue that when God creates mankind, He surrenders His control over to them, and He provides and grants them with absolute freedom, because He wants them to enjoy full free will. It was an attempt by the Mu'tazilites to defend

God's justice by saying that God, in any shape or form, does not coerce His creatures. Instead, the creatures themselves are the creators and architects of their own behaviors and deeds, and God does not interfere with them at all.

The Mu'tazilites have had a long battle with their opponents, the Ash'arites (Coercionists), who believe that it is only God who is the Creator of all of our behavior and deeds, and that man is nothing but a robot who follows instructions. The old school of Ash'arites tried to defend God's monotheism against the Mu'tazilites, but both groups fell into grave error. The Mu'tazilites, when defending God's Justice, compromised His monotheism; and on the other hand, the Ash'arites, while preserving God's monotheism, encroached on His Divine Justice. Of course, contemporary Ash'arites realized their deviant opinion and mitigated their tone. Their contemporary scholars argue that man enjoys some freedom, and he can choose his own path in this life. At the time of the Imamate of Imam al-Sadiq, when the philosophical schools started to surface, the School of the *Ahlulbayt* was the only school which reconciled between protecting God's monotheism and His Divine Justice.

لا جبر ولا تفويض وإنما أمر بين أمرين

> "It is neither absolute force, nor absolute free will. Rather, it is a matter between the two."[9]

The Imams of *Ahlulbayt* assert that although man is free and independent, and enjoys freedom of choice, this does not negate the fact that God, the Almighty, has an overall power over him. Thus, man is not completely independent from God, neither in the beginning of their journey (*huduth*), nor in its continuation

[9] *Bihaar al-Anwaar*, Al-Majlisi, vol. 75, pg. 354.

(*baqaa'*). In every moment and every time, man is in need of help and sustenance from the Divine (*al-Faydh al-Ilaahi*).

The Legislative Relegation (*Al-Tafweedh al-Tashriee*)

Al-Tafweedh al-Tashriee implies that God has left His right to legislation and put other beings in charge of law making.

Al-Tafweedh al-Tashriee in the Pre-Islamic Era

Before discussing the meaning of *Al-Tafweedh al-Tashriee* among Muslim scholars, we should review similar cases in the pre-Islamic era. The Qur'an states the following regarding the pre-Islamic communities:

ٱتَّخَذُوٓاْ أَحْبَارَهُمْ وَرُهْبَٰنَهُمْ أَرْبَابًا مِّن دُونِ ٱللَّهِ

> They have taken their rabbis and monks as lords apart from God.[10]

How did the Jews and Christians mentioned in this verse take their rabbis, priests, and monks as lords? The Jews and Christians offered absolute submission and excessive obedience to them, which is impermissible. Furthermore, Prophet Muhammad explains that this submission is impermissible because the rabbis, priests, and monks forbade what God permitted, and permitted what God forbade. This is considered a form of worship towards them, rather than to God.

There is a fine line between acts of monotheism and polytheism. One must not conflate the two. Listening to a religious authority who speaks on behalf of God, and whose information is based on authentic narrations is legitimate; whereas a religious authority who speaks on behalf of one's own desires or on behalf of Satan is considered illegitimate.

---

[10] Qur'an, Surah al-Tawbah (9), verse 31.

It should be clarified that the Prophet's role as an intermediary between people and God, as in verse 4:64 (further elaborated on in Chapter 10), still meant that the people were seeking forgiveness from God, not the Prophet himself, as the Prophet was acting like an intercessor for the people to God.

وَيَعْبُدُونَ مِن دُونِ ٱللَّهِ مَا لَا يَضُرُّهُمْ وَلَا يَنفَعُهُمْ وَيَقُولُونَ هَٰٓؤُلَآءِ شُفَعَٰٓؤُنَا عِندَ ٱللَّهِ ۚ قُلْ أَتُنَبِّـُٔونَ ٱللَّهَ بِمَا لَا يَعْلَمُ فِى ٱلسَّمَٰوَٰتِ وَلَا فِى ٱلْأَرْضِ ۚ سُبْحَٰنَهُۥ وَتَعَٰلَىٰ عَمَّا يُشْرِكُونَ

> And they worship apart from God, which neither harms them nor benefits them. And they say: "These are our intercessors with God." Say: "Would you inform God about something in the heavens or on the earth that He does not know? Glory be to Him and exalted is He above the partners they ascribe!"[11]

The polytheists used to worship their idols, and seek their intercession. Monotheists on the other hand, do not worship any vicegerent of God, nor do they believe in their divinity. They only seek their intercession with the permission of God. The legitimate vicegerents are entities who are recognized by God, but cannot intercede without His permission.

Al-Tafweedh al-Tashriee during the Islamic Era

The meaning of *Al-Tafweedh al-Tashriee* in the Islamic era developed into the concept of God transferring the power of legislation in matters of religion to the Prophet, and the Prophet in turn, bequeathing this power to the Imams after him. There

[11] Qur'ans, Surah Yunus (10), verse 18.

are two groups of scholars who reflect on the concept of *Al-Tafweedh al-Tashriee.*

The first group believes that God gave authority to His Messenger to create law, not as an absolute *Al-Tafweedh*, but as a type of conditional *Al-Tafweedh* by God's approval, and that the Prophet did actually introduce religious laws to his community which are called *al-Sunnah al-Nabawiyyah.*

A demonstration of this Prophetic legislation is the canonical prayers: when they were first introduced by God, they consisted of two units for each of the five daily prayers. It was the Prophet who added two more units to the noon (*dhuhr*), afternoon (*asr*), and night (*isha*) prayers, and one unit to the evening (*maghrib*) prayer. Thus, the total units of the canonical prayers became seventeen, and the total for the recommended ones was thirty-four, double that of the canonical. This *hadith* has been mentioned in *Al-Kafi*, and the Arabic version is below.[12]

سمعت أبا عبد الله عليه السلام يقول لبعض أصحاب قيس الماصر: إن الله عز وجل أدب نبيه فأحسن أدبه فلما أكمل له الأدب قال: " إنك لعلى خلق عظيم "، ثم فوض إليه أمر الدين والأمة ليسوس عباده، فقال عز وجل: " ما آتاكم الرسول فخذوه وما نهاكم عنه فانتهوا " وإن رسول الله صلى الله عليه وآله كان مسددا موفقا مؤيدا بروح القدس، لا يزل ولا يخطئ في شئ مما يسوس به الخلق، فتأدب بآداب الله ثم إن الله عز وجل فرض الصلاة ركعتين، ركعتين عشر ركعات فأضاف رسول الله صلى الله عليه وآله إلى الوكعتين ركعتين وإلى المغرب ركعة فصارت عديل الفريضة لا يجوز تركهن إلا في سفر وأفرد الوكعة في المغرب فتركها

[12] *Al-Kafi*, Al-Kulayni, vol. 1, pg. 266.

قائمة في السفر والحضر فأجاز الله عز وجل له ذلك فصارت
الفريضة سبع عشرة ركعة، ثم سن رسول الله صلى الله عليه وآله
النوافل أربعا وثلاثين ركعة مثلي الفريضة

Thus, Muslim jurists distinguish between what was introduced by God which is called *fareedhah*, and that which was introduced by the Prophet which is called *Sunnah*. *Sunnah* contains mandatory actions (such as the extra units of prayer mentioned above), as well as recommended ones (such as the optional prayers called *al-nawaafil*).

In the dietary system, the Prophet also introduced laws. While God forbade wine (see Qur'an 5:90) in which God says: "O you who believe! Wine, and gambling, and idols, and divining arrows are but a means of defilement, of Satan's doing. So avoid it, that haply you may prosper," the Apostle of God added to this prohibition every intoxicant. These Prophetic legislations have roots in the Qur'an, and followers of Islam are commanded by God to follow what their Prophet legislated for them. The Qur'an stresses in Surah al-Hashr, chapter 59, verse 7 that: "Whatever the Messenger gives you, take it; and whatever he forbids you from, forgo that."

The second group of scholars who discuss *Al-Tafweedh al-Tashriee,* state that legislation is a right that belongs solely to God, and no one shares that right with Him. He may, if He wills, bestow that right to whomsoever He is pleased with, and there is nothing wrong with that rationally; however, even though this matter is possible in the theoretical stage (*maqaam al-ithbat*), it has not been proven in the practical stage (*maqaam al-thubut*). Therefore, this group of Shia Muslim scholars do not recognize the Prophet to be a legislator, but merely a transferor or conveyor of God's Legislation to the people. Among those scholars are contemporary scholars such as Sayed Gulpaygani and Sheikh Subhani of Qum Seminary.

Refuting the Concept of Relegation

After this quick review of the different opinions of scholars, we conclude that the entire concept of *Al-Tafweedh,* with its breadth of meaning of God giving absolute and independent legislative and administrative power to His vicegerents, is rejected by the Imams of *Ahlulbayt.* God does not delegate other beings to carry out His duties as such, because this kind of belief would compromise the Self-Sufficiency of God, as it promotes the idea that God is not able to perform His duties and puts someone else in charge.

The only Sovereign Power in this universe is God. He is eternally in charge of the affairs of the universe. He neither abdicates His Throne, nor resigns from His Post, nor does He surrender His Power or Authority.

God, at certain times, gives some level of power and authority to specific personalities to perform miracles. He entrusts the power of attorney regarding certain matters of life (*al-Wilaayah al-Takwiniyyah*), and legislation (*al-Wilaayah al-Tashri'iyyah*) (see verse 7 of Surah al-Hashr mentioned above) to the Prophets and Imams, however He is still in complete charge of supervising and controlling all situations. The vicegerents of God are not independent caretakers of the universe. They are His servants, working strictly by His orders and following His commands. Nothing in this universe can take place without God's awareness, presence, and permission (see examples in the Qur'an: 2:60, 3:49, 12:93 & 98, 20:77, 21:81, 34:12, 38:36 & 39, and many more).

So why did God need vicegerents for His Mission in the first place?

With regard to sending the Prophets and Imams, God did not make them His partners, associates, or equals. He has sent them as guides for His creations to bring them the scriptures, and be role models for mankind. They have been endowed with powers and authority of universal magnitude in regards to religious matters, and God occasionally provided His vicegerents with metaphysical and extraordinary powers, to support their cause and facilitate their missions.

God sometimes empowers His vicegerents to undertake extraordinary acts of healing and providing provision, which is different from the concept of *Al-Tafweedh*. The following two sections provide some examples of how God empowers His vicegerents.

The Power of Healing

An aspect of God's Divine Power and Authority is His ability to heal. When it comes to health and healing, the Qur'an says:

وَإِذَا مَرِضْتُ فَهُوَ يَشْفِينِ

> And when I am ill, it is He Who heals me.[13]

All healing comes from God, and there can be no cure without God's permission. However, He may choose a spiritual figure, such as a doctor or an object, to heal someone. One might say that it is blasphemous to call anyone else a healer besides God. But by looking at the Qur'an, one will find that God Himself has delegated the ability to heal to other figures, as well as objects. God mentions in the Qur'an how He has given honey the ability to cure people.

[13] Qur'an, Surah al-Shu'ara (26), verse 80.

فِيهِ شِفَآءٌ لِّلنَّاسِ

> Wherein [honey] there is healing for mankind.[14]

وَنُنَزِّلُ مِنَ ٱلْقُرْءَانِ مَا هُوَ شِفَآءٌ وَرَحْمَةٌ لِّلْمُؤْمِنِينَ

> And We send down of the Qur'an that which is a cure and a mercy for the believers.[15]

The Qur'an is not only a source of mercy for mankind, but it is a source of spiritual healing as well. Therefore, it is not blasphemous to look at other figures or things for healing when one believes that ultimately all healing in the universe comes only from God's permission. Once a Prophet got sick and refused to visit a doctor unless God directly bestowed healing upon him. God responded to him that He will never cure him unless he visits a doctor, since this is the system of God.[16] It will be elaborated later on how material and spiritual elements combined, can produce a result.

Providing Provision

Another aspect of Divine Power and Authority is the ability to provide provision and sustenance to all creatures. This provision can be in the form of wealth, food, shelter, job, security, family, etc.

إِنَّ ٱللَّهَ هُوَ ٱلرَّزَّاقُ ذُو ٱلْقُوَّةِ ٱلْمَتِينُ

> Truly God is the Provider, the Possessor of Strength, the Firm.[17]

---

[14] Qur'an, Surah al-Nahl (16), verse 69.
[15] Qur'an, Surah al-Isra (17), verse 82.
[16] *Bihaar al-Anwaar*, Al-Majlisi, vol. 59, pg. 66.
[17] Qur'an, Surah al-Dhaariyat (51), verse 58.

It must be noted that God is the ultimate Sustainer and sole Provider of all sustenance to the universe, and He provides however much He wills.

وَمَا نُنَزِّلُهُۥٓ إِلَّا بِقَدَرٍ مَّعْلُومٍ

> And We do not send it down except in a known (and specified) measure.[18]

However, God may delegate the ability to provide sustenance to the breadwinners or others in the community to help provide their families with sustenance.

وَٱرْزُقُوهُمْ فِيهَا وَٱكْسُوهُمْ

> But provide them their sustenance with it, and clothe them.[19]

It should not be considered blasphemous if someone is described as the breadwinner or sustainer (*raaziq*) of one's family. That person has been delegated by God to sustain and provide for their family with His permission. This does not undermine God's Authority to sustain. It should be noted though that a person's ability to sustain oneself or family depends entirely on God, however God does not depend on anyone at all. He is the One who inspires mercy and care into the hearts of His servants so that they can provide for their families and communities.

In the supplication which is recommended to recite on the day of 'Arafah, Imam Hussain states that an example of God's mercy can be envisioned in a mother's heart: "It is You Who protected (me)" and "It is You Who gave me into the charge of merciful mothers." Providers and caregivers could be a mother, nanny, doctor, nurse, etc.

---

[18] Qur'an, Surah al-Hijr (15), verse 21.
[19] Qur'an, Surah al-Nisaa (4), verse 5.

God protects and shields man against his enemies as well; not directly, but through soldiers and advocates. Therefore, a person cannot attribute victory to oneself alone.

فَلَمْ تَقْتُلُوهُمْ وَلَٰكِنَّ ٱللَّهَ قَتَلَهُمْ ۚ وَمَا رَمَيْتَ إِذْ رَمَيْتَ وَلَٰكِنَّ ٱللَّهَ رَمَىٰ وَلِيُبْلِيَ ٱلْمُؤْمِنِينَ مِنْهُ بَلَآءً حَسَنًا ۚ

> And you did not slay them, but God slew them; and you threw not when you threw, but it was God who threw that He might try the believers with a beautiful trial from Him.[20]

Man can only protect himself through God's help and aid. God reminds the Prophet that it was not the Muslims who defended themselves against their enemies in the battle of Uhud, but rather it was God. Without His Power and Permission, no one would have been able to achieve victory.

A man must never be arrogant enough to believe that his success is self-made. One is only successful because God chose for him to be successful by providing him with His help and guidance.

وَمَا بِكُم مِّن نِّعْمَةٍ فَمِنَ ٱللَّهِ

> And whatever blessing you have, it is from God.[21]

It is imperative to note that one's success can be determined by the choices that one makes in how to act upon the free will that is granted by the Almighty. If one takes advantage of God's help and works hard in His way, then success will be inevitable. If one does not do this, then it is because one chooses to be indifferent. However, it must never be forgotten that God is always there to

---

[20] Qur'an, Surah al-Anfaal (8), verse 17.

[21] Qur'an, Surah al-Nahl (16), verse 53.

help those who seek help from Him, despite the failures that are incurred on the way.

10

The Supernatural Power of God's Vicegerents

وَمَا كَانَ لِرَسُولٍ أَن يَأْتِيَ بِـَٔايَةٍ إِلَّا بِإِذْنِ ٱللَّهِ

> And it was not for a messenger to bring a sign except by the permission of God.[1]

[1] Qur'an, Surah Ghaafir (40), verse 78.

The discussion about supernatural abilities that God bestowed upon His vicegerents remains an ongoing and controversial topic within the scope of monotheism. One may ask: "How do vicegerents of God have any supernatural abilities?" Through different chapters and various stories, the Qur'an illustrates that God bestowed certain powers upon His vicegerents in order for them to perform miracles that would be a tool to help them in their missions. The core of the debate among Muslim scholars is whether these supernatural powers of the Prophets could also be bestowed on others or not; and whether a vicegerent after his death, can continue to provide his blessings.

Although God has the jurisdiction to share His powers with whomsoever He wills, a vicegerent cannot perform a miracle without the permission of God. Some scholars debate whether vicegerents have access to supernatural powers that would bring about changes in the universe. To answer this question, one must realize that there are two types of powers a vicegerent may be believed to possess: either a power independent of God, or one dependent upon Him.

If one believes that a vicegerent possesses natural or supernatural abilities that are independent of God, then such a belief is invalid, as it undermines the idea of monotheism. However, if one believes that a vicegerent possesses abilities that are dependent on and derived from God, then such a belief is consistent with Qur'anic views and is considered an act of monotheism.

Knocking at His vicegerents' doors, provides access to God and His material and spiritual provisions and bounties. The Qur'an encourages people to seek the means to receive the bounties of God:

وَٱبْتَغُوٓاْ إِلَيْهِ ٱلْوَسِيلَةَ

> And seek the means to (approach) Him.[1]

The phrase "seek the means" in the above verse connotes different ways and channels. These could be in the shape of acts of worship, giving in charity, and acts of wholesomeness, or seeking the help and intercession of the Prophets or Imams. Such intercession does not rest on the vicegerents only during their lives. The powers which God bestowed upon them do not cease after they die, they transcend material boundaries to reach all people at all times. Therefore, the death of the vicegerents does not render their guidance, blessings, or intercession useless.

The Qur'an emphasizes that the prophets were human beings, carrying human desires and sentiments, but with a better ability to control them. Thus, they were entitled to receive revelation, special abilities, and powers by God to perform supernatural work in His way.

قُلْ إِنَّمَآ أَنَا۠ بَشَرٌ مِّثْلُكُمْ يُوحَىٰٓ إِلَىَّ أَنَّمَآ إِلَٰهُكُمْ إِلَٰهٌ وَٰحِدٌ

> Say: "I am only a human being like you. It is revealed unto me that your God is one God.[2]

Since the prophets were true servants of God, He bestowed upon them honorary titles such as: "the friend of God" (*Khalilullah*) for Abraham; "the one who converses with God" (*Kalimullah*) for Moses; "the spirit of God" (*Ruhullah*) for Jesus; and "the beloved of God" (*Habibullah*) for Prophet Muhammad. Below are various examples of prophets who were approached by their followers to be mediums of survival between them and God, beginning with the story of Prophet Noah.

---

[1] Qur'an, Surah al-Ma'idah (5), verse 35.
[2] Qur'an, Surah al-Kahf (18), verse 110.

Prophet Noah and His Son

The story of Prophet Noah and his son represents an example of how a Prophet can be a means of salvation for his family and community. Noah begged his son to embark on his ark with him, but his son refused.

يَٰبُنَيَّ ٱرۡكَب مَّعَنَا

> "O my son! Embark with us."[3]

قَالَ سَـَٔاوِيٓ إِلَىٰ جَبَلٖ يَعۡصِمُنِي مِنَ ٱلۡمَآءِۚ قَالَ لَا عَاصِمَ ٱلۡيَوۡمَ مِنۡ أَمۡرِ ٱللَّهِ إِلَّا مَن رَّحِمَۚ وَحَالَ بَيۡنَهُمَا ٱلۡمَوۡجُ فَكَانَ مِنَ ٱلۡمُغۡرَقِينَ

> He (the son) said: "I shall take refuge on a mountain; it will protect me from the water." He (Prophet Noah) said: "There is no protector on this day from the Command of God except for the one upon whom He has Mercy." And the waves came between them, and he was among the drowned.[4]

Noah's son refused to embark on his father's ark and insisted that he would be safe if he climbed the mountain summit. Although Noah warned his son that the summit would not be safe from the flood, his son kept insisting and ultimately he drowned. Through this story, God teaches us that although He is the main Saver and Protector of humanity, He will exercise certain things through human means. Prophet Noah steered the ark of salvation for his community; and similarly, Prophet Muhammad referred to his family as the ark of salvation for all mankind:

---

[3] Qur'an, Surah Hud (11), verse 42.
[4] Qur'an, Surah Hud (11), verse 43.

إنما مثل أهل بيتي فيكم كمثل سفينة نوح من ركبها نجا، ومن تخلف عنها هلك

> The similitude of my family among you is like the ark of Noah: whoever embarks on it will be saved, and whoever stays behind it will perish.[5]

Prophet Solomon

Prophet Solomon, even though he was a human being, had the supernatural ability to control the winds.

وَلِسُلَيْمَٰنَ ٱلرِّيحَ عَاصِفَةً تَجْرِى بِأَمْرِهِۦٓ

> And to Solomon, (We subjected) the wind, blowing violently: it ran by his command.[6]

It was God who gave that ability to this Prophet to demonstrate to the people at his time that he was a Messenger of God. Apart from being able to control the winds, Prophet Solomon also had an army of *jinn*, animals, and insects under his command.

وَحُشِرَ لِسُلَيْمَٰنَ جُنُودُهُۥ مِنَ ٱلْجِنِّ وَٱلْإِنسِ وَٱلطَّيْرِ فَهُمْ يُوزَعُونَ

> And gathered for Solomon were his hosts of *jinn* and men and birds, and they were marshaled [in ordered ranks].[7]

وَتَفَقَّدَ ٱلطَّيْرَ فَقَالَ مَا لِىَ لَآ أَرَى ٱلْهُدْهُدَ أَمْ كَانَ مِنَ ٱلْغَآئِبِينَ

> And he surveyed the birds and said: "How is it that I do not see the hoopoe? Or is he among those who are absent?[8]

[5] *Kanz al-Ummal,* trad. 34,169.
[6] Qur'an, Surah al-Anbiya (21), verse 81.
[7] Qur'an, Surah al-Naml (27), verse 17.
[8] Qur'an, Surah al-Naml (27), verse 20.

Prophets Jacob and Joseph

The most striking story of prophets possessing supernatural powers is that of Jacob and his son Joseph.

ٱذْهَبُوا۟ بِقَمِيصِى هَـٰذَا فَأَلْقُوهُ عَلَىٰ وَجْهِ أَبِى يَأْتِ بَصِيرًا وَأْتُونِى
بِأَهْلِكُمْ أَجْمَعِينَ ۝ وَلَمَّا فَصَلَتِ ٱلْعِيرُ قَالَ أَبُوهُمْ إِنِّى لَأَجِدُ
رِيحَ يُوسُفَ ۖ لَوْلَآ أَن تُفَنِّدُونِ

> Take this shirt of mine and cast it upon my father's face; he will regain his sight. And bring me your family, all together." And as the caravan set off (from Egypt), their father said: "Truly I sense the scent of Joseph, if you think me not senile!"[9]

فَلَمَّآ أَن جَآءَ ٱلْبَشِيرُ أَلْقَىٰهُ عَلَىٰ وَجْهِهِۦ فَٱرْتَدَّ بَصِيرًا

> And when the bearer of glad tidings came, he cast it upon his face and he was restored to sight.[10]

Prophet Jacob had lost his eyesight due to his grief over the separation from his son for 40 years. When his brothers came to Egypt, Prophet Joseph told them to take his shirt and cast it upon his father's eyes. When the shirt of Joseph was cast upon the face of Jacob, he regained his vision. Joseph carried out this act with God's permission. An interesting thought about this event is that God did not command Jacob, who was also a Prophet, to use his own shirt, but sent His miracle through his son's shirt. This is a sign indicating that supernatural powers are bestowed upon special people by God's choice and only with His permission.

[9] Qur'an, Surah Yusuf (12), verses 93-94.
[10] Qur'an, Surah Yusuf (12), verse 96.

Prophet Moses and the Israelites

وَلَمَّا وَقَعَ عَلَيۡهِمُ ٱلرِّجۡزُ قَالُواْ يَٰمُوسَى ٱدۡعُ لَنَا رَبَّكَ بِمَا عَهِدَ عِندَكَۖ لَئِن كَشَفۡتَ عَنَّا ٱلرِّجۡزَ لَنُؤۡمِنَنَّ لَكَ وَلَنُرۡسِلَنَّ مَعَكَ بَنِيٓ إِسۡرَٰٓءِيلَ

> And when the torment came down upon them, they said: "O Moses! Call upon your Lord for us by the covenant He has made with you. If you lift this torment from us, we shall surely believe in you, and we shall surely send forth the Children of Israel with you."[11]

Another example of God granting His Prophets supernatural abilities is the story of Prophet Moses. When the people of Pharaoh continued their persecution of the children of Israel, God sent punishments upon them. Unable to bear the punishment of God, the people of Pharaoh went to Moses to intercede for them and ask God to remove His chastisements from them. Moses interceded for them and God removed His punishment.

فَأَوۡحَيۡنَآ إِلَىٰ مُوسَىٰٓ أَنِ ٱضۡرِب بِّعَصَاكَ ٱلۡبَحۡرَۖ فَٱنفَلَقَ فَكَانَ كُلُّ فِرۡقٖ كَٱلطَّوۡدِ ٱلۡعَظِيمِ

> Then We revealed unto Moses: "Strike the sea with your staff," and it parted, and each part was like a great mountain.[12]

When Prophet Moses and the children of Israel were being chased by Pharaoh's army, God commanded Moses to strike the

---

[11] Qur'an, Surah al-A'raaf (7), verse 134.
[12] Qur'an, Surah al-Shu'ara (26), verse 63.

sea with his rod which caused the sea to split, each part into a towering mountain. This opened a passageway through the sea for them to cross to safety. It must be noted that Moses did not have the ability to carry out this miracle on his own. He was only able to perform this miracle because God gave him the power and ability to do so.

When Moses took his people to the Sinai Desert, they asked him to call upon his Lord to provide them with different types of food.

فَٱدْعُ لَنَا رَبَّكَ يُخْرِجْ لَنَا مِمَّا تُنۢبِتُ ٱلْأَرْضُ مِنۢ بَقْلِهَا وَقِثَّآئِهَا وَفُومِهَا وَعَدَسِهَا وَبَصَلِهَا

> "Call upon your Lord for us that He may bring forth for us some of what the earth grows: its herbs, its cucumbers, its garlic, its lentils, and its onions."[13]

The people of Prophet Moses did not commit a sin by asking him and not calling upon God directly. In fact, they called upon God by calling upon Moses. This Prophet was only a vicegerent of God, and all of his actions were dependent entirely on the permission of God.

Prophet Jesus

Prophet Jesus enjoyed the supernatural ability, bestowed upon him by God, of creating beings from clay, healing the sick, and bringing the dead back to life, as can be seen in the following verse of the Qur'an:

[13] Qur'an, Surah al-Baqarah (2), verse 61.

أَنِّيٓ أَخۡلُقُ لَكُم مِّنَ ٱلطِّينِ كَهَيۡـَٔةِ ٱلطَّيۡرِ فَأَنفُخُ فِيهِ فَيَكُونُ
طَيۡرَۢا بِإِذۡنِ ٱللَّهِۖ وَأُبۡرِئُ ٱلۡأَكۡمَهَ وَٱلۡأَبۡرَصَ وَأُحۡيِ ٱلۡمَوۡتَىٰ بِإِذۡنِ
ٱللَّهِ

> I will create for you out of clay the shape of a bird, then I will breathe into it, and it will be a bird by the permission of God. And I will heal the blind and the leper, and give life to the dead by the permission of God.[14]

Jesus told his community that the only reason he was able to create real beings from clay, cure the sick, and resurrect the dead was because of the permission given to him by God. Prophets cannot even do any good or bad to themselves without the authorization of God. The final Prophet of Islam was commanded to say to the people:

قُل لَّآ أَمۡلِكُ لِنَفۡسِي ضَرّٗا وَلَا نَفۡعًا إِلَّا مَا شَآءَ ٱللَّهُ

> Say: "I have no power over what harm or benefit may come to me except as God wills."[15]

Prophet Muhammad and His Family

God forgives sinners who wrong themselves and come to Prophet Muhammad to ask for his intercession for forgiveness from God.

---

[14] Qur'an, Surah Ale Imraan (3), verse 49.
[15] Qur'an, Surah Yunus (10), verse 49.

وَمَآ أَرۡسَلۡنَا مِن رَّسُولٍ إِلَّا لِيُطَاعَ بِإِذۡنِ ٱللَّهِۚ وَلَوۡ أَنَّهُمۡ إِذ ظَّلَمُوٓاْ
أَنفُسَهُمۡ جَآءُوكَ فَٱسۡتَغۡفَرُواْ ٱللَّهَ وَٱسۡتَغۡفَرَ لَهُمُ ٱلرَّسُولُ لَوَجَدُواْ
ٱللَّهَ تَوَّابًا رَّحِيمًا

> And if, when they had wronged themselves, they had come to you and asked forgiveness of God, and the Messenger had asked forgiveness for them then they would surely have found God Oft-Forgiving, All-Merciful.[16]

God also commanded the Prophet to spiritually bless his community, for it had a healing power for them.

وَصَلِّ عَلَيۡهِمۡۖ إِنَّ صَلَوٰتَكَ سَكَنٌ لَّهُمۡ

> And bless them. Truly your blessings are a comfort for them.[17]

Furthermore, the Prophet and his successors are considered to be the main gate and connection to God.

مَّن يُطِعِ ٱلرَّسُولَ فَقَدۡ أَطَاعَ ٱللَّهَۖ وَمَن تَوَلَّىٰ فَمَآ أَرۡسَلۡنَٰكَ عَلَيۡهِمۡ
حَفِيظًا

> Whosoever obeys the Messenger obeys God, and as for those who turn away, We have not sent you as a guardian over them.[18]

The reason why the above verse emphasizes that to obey the Prophet is to obey God, and to disobey the Prophet is to disobey God is because the only way to truly follow God and know His commands is through His Prophet.

---

[16] Qur'an, Surah al-Nisaa (4), verse 64.
[17] Qur'an, Surah al-Tawbah (9), verse 103.
[18] Qur'an, Surah al-Nisaa (4), verse 80.

Seeking the intercession of the Prophet and his progeny is one of the fundamentals of Islamic teachings and practices. Even though a seeker may directly go to God anytime without any intermediaries, *Tawassul*, or calling upon the Prophet and his family, will expedite the answer. There are pathways which lead to God, and the main pathway to Him are the prophets, especially Prophet Muhammad and his family.

If one seeks salvation, it can be done through the ark of the family of the Prophet, as Prophet Muhammad himself said:

مثل أهل بيتي فيكم كمثل سفينة نوح من ركبها نجا ومن تخلف عنها غرق وهوى

> The parable of my family among you [Muslims] is like the ark of Noah. Whoever embarked on it was saved, and whoever refused to embark on it drowned and perished.[19]

Can Prophets and Imams still Help People after their Deaths?

The Prophets of God are buried in various places: Adam, Noah, Hud, and Saleh are in Najaf; Abraham is in Hebron; Ishmael is buried in Mecca; Moses lies in Jericho; David and Solomon are in Jerusalem; Zachariah is in Aleppo; John the Baptist is buried in Damascus; Prophet Muhammad was laid to rest in Medina; and many other graves can be found in different places. Is it permissible to visit these graves and ask for their intercession?

A group of Muslims believe that Prophets cannot help themselves after their death, let alone others, and that no one has the right to call upon them for intercession, as they are dead. They describe the act of calling upon the Prophets as an act of blasphemy. However, with deep reflection on the Qur'an, one

---

[19] *Al-'Amaali*, Al-Sadooq, pg. 341; *Al-'Amaali*, Al-Tusi, pg. 60.

will realize that God did not grant supernatural abilities or power of intercession to His Prophets only when they were alive; He granted the same privileges to them even after they left this world. Divinely given powers of Prophets and Imams do not expire with their death; rather these benefits continue to be with them until the Day of Judgment. The Qur'an also falsifies the notion of martyrs and people of God being classified as dead:

وَلَا تَحْسَبَنَّ ٱلَّذِينَ قُتِلُواْ فِي سَبِيلِ ٱللَّهِ أَمْوَٰتًاۚ بَلْ أَحْيَآءٌ عِندَ رَبِّهِمْ يُرْزَقُونَ

> And do not think of those slain in the way of God to be dead. Rather, they are alive with their Lord, and they have provision.[20]

وَلَا تَقُولُواْ لِمَن يُقْتَلُ فِي سَبِيلِ ٱللَّهِ أَمْوَٰتٌۚ بَلْ أَحْيَآءٌ وَلَٰكِن لَّا تَشْعُرُونَ

> And say not of those who are slain in the way of God, "They are dead." Nay, they are alive, but you are unaware.[21]

If the Qur'an considers an ordinary Muslim who was killed for the cause of God to be spiritually alive, then how can the Prophet and his family, who were not only martyrs, but whose rank also surpasses that of all other martyrs, be considered dead?

The concept that death is not considered to be the end of life, is an instrumental one within the Holy Qur'an. Death is nothing more than a mere transition from one abode to another. Upon death, a virtuous human soul enters a new abode which is higher and more sublime than the physical and earthly one.

---

[20] Qur'an, Surah Ale Imraan (3), verse 169.
[21] Qur'an, Surah al-Baqarah (2), verse 154.

With the permission of God, the soul of the Prophet, his family, the Imams, the vicegerents, and other intimate servants of God (the *Awliyaa)*, can discern our petitions and prayers. Their passing away from this temporary world does not negate their ability to intercede for other people. One can visit their shrines or speak to them from miles away. This is not an act of blasphemy, but an act of monotheism, because these intimate servants of God do not carry out any action on their own, but solely by God's permission. Thus, with the permission of God, they respond to the requests of people.

Going through the gates of God's vicegerents also helps us to understand and realize their status and worthiness with God. It is a way of paying tribute and respect to them, which in turn, demonstrates respect and humility towards God. If someone has a difficulty that they want to escape from, they can ask for the intercession of any of these chosen prophets and Imams, and God can grant them their wish if He wills.

Among the Shia Muslims, Imam Hussain is tremendously popular, since he stands as a symbol of resistance against tyranny. Some opponents may argue that calling out "Ya Hussain", which means "O Hussain", undermines the belief in God's monotheism. However, calling out "Ya Hussain" is neither blasphemous, nor it is an action of apostacy, due to the fact that Imam Hussain is the vicegerent of God, and not in any way parallel to Him. It is God who gave him and other *Awliyaa* the power of intercession. Therefore, calling on him is an act of monotheism, as Hussain is an agent of God and a path to Him.

Prophet Muhammad used to call upon Archangel Gabriel for help, knowing that Gabriel does not do anything without God's permission. In Islamic tradition, a pious believer may achieve a higher status than an angel, because a believer has free will and desire to commit a sin, but chooses not to in obedience to God;

whereas an angel has neither free will nor desire to commit any sin. If an average believer's status becomes higher than an angel when exercising self-control and self-restraint, would then a *wali* like Imam Hussain not be worthy of the highest level of guidance and salvation?

Seeking Help from God through Others

Does calling upon someone other than the Almighty for help strip a person away from being a true Muslim? A concise response to this question is provided in the Qur'an. It mentions that a Prophet of God called upon a person for help without the intention of believing in that person's divinity. This is what the Qur'an mentions about Prophet Joseph:

وَقَالَ لِلَّذِى ظَنَّ أَنَّهُۥ نَاجٍ مِّنْهُمَا اذْكُرْنِى عِندَ رَبِّكَ فَأَنسَاهُ الشَّيْطَانُ ذِكْرَ رَبِّهِۦ فَلَبِثَ فِى السِّجْنِ بِضْعَ سِنِينَ

> And he said to the one of them whom he knew would be saved: "Mention me to your lord." But Satan caused him to forget to make mention to his lord. So he (Joseph) remained in prison for several years.[22]

It has been established that to call upon someone for help while believing that the said person is powerful in their own way and not dependant on God is an act of blasphemy. On the contrary, to call upon someone for help while believing that the said person is only able to help because of the ability given to them by God is a pure act of monotheism.

When Joseph was in prison, he shared a cell with two other inmates. One of them was sentenced to death, while the other was about to be released. To the inmate who was about to be

---

[22] Qur'an, Surah Yusuf (12), verse 42.

released, Joseph requested to have his case mentioned to the king. The inmate forgot to mention his case to the king, and as a result, Joseph remained in prison for several more years. Was Joseph's request to this inmate deemed to be inappropriate because he did not ask for help directly from God?

مَا كَانَ لَنَا أَن نُّشْرِكَ بِاللَّهِ مِن شَيْءٍ

> It is not for us to ascribe any partners with God.[23]

Joseph was an absolute monotheist who did not worship anyone or anything else except for God. The Qur'an describes him as being a chosen servant:

إِنَّهُ مِنْ عِبَادِنَا الْمُخْلَصِينَ

> Truly he was among Our chosen servants.[24]

Never once did Prophet Joseph look to anyone or anything else for help besides God. A chosen servant is one whose heart does not get attached to anything else but God. Joseph was further described as being given the hidden knowledge of things.

وَكَذَٰلِكَ يَجْتَبِيكَ رَبُّكَ وَيُعَلِّمُكَ مِن تَأْوِيلِ الْأَحَادِيثِ

> And thus shall your Lord choose you, and teach you the interpretation of events.[25]

With such a caliber and a heart knowing no one but God, Joseph cannot be accused of having hope in anything other than God. Joseph's relationship with God would not be compromised merely to request the freed inmate to bring his case to the king in hopes that the king would realize his innocence and pardon him.

---

[23] Qur'an, Surah Yusuf (12), verse 38.
[24] Qur'an, Surah Yusuf (12), verse 24.
[25] Qur'an, Surah Yusuf (12), verse 6.

Divine Grace

يَٰٓأَيُّهَا ٱلنَّاسُ أَنتُمُ ٱلْفُقَرَآءُ إِلَى ٱللَّهِ ۖ وَٱللَّهُ هُوَ ٱلْغَنِىُّ ٱلْحَمِيدُ ۝ إِن يَشَأْ يُذْهِبْكُمْ وَيَأْتِ بِخَلْقٍ جَدِيدٍ ۝ وَمَا ذَٰلِكَ عَلَى ٱللَّهِ بِعَزِيزٍ

> O mankind! You are needful of God; and He is the Self-Sufficient, the Praised. If He wills, He can remove you and bring forth a new creation. And that is no great matter for God.[26]

People who argue that help should be sought directly from God without His legitimate intermediaries, should reflect on the fact that Muslims stand firm in the belief that all power belongs solely to God. He is Self-Sufficient and does not depend on anyone, while everyone and everything else depends upon Him. The universe is able to function only because of God's Grace. Without this Grace, the universe would be incapacitated and non-functional. God is the source of all life, and everything that functions in this universe is a result of His will. However, as demonstrated in the examples of the Prophets, He gives permission to His legitimate intermediaries to perform certain miracles and seek intercession for people. God executes His commands through these intermediaries.

> Once, the scholar and sage, Bahlool son of Amr al-Sayrafi al-Kufi (d. 190 H., Baghdad) met the Abbasid caliph Haroon, who exhibited extraordinary pride about his kingdom's vastness and strength. Bahlool said to him: "Imagine if you are locked alone in a room with no way out, and you are extremely thirsty. How much of your

[26] Qur'an, Surah Faatir (35), verses 15-17.

> wealth are you willing to give for a cup of water?" The caliph responded: "Half of my fortune." Bahlool continued: "Fine, then imagine that you drank the water, and now you need to empty your bladder, but you cannot do that. How much of your wealth are you willing to give to empty your bladder?" The caliph replied: "The other half of my fortune." Bahlool responded: "Your majesty, your entire kingdom and its wealth equals only a drink of water and its release, so why be so arrogant?"[27]

The above story summons the reality about human weakness and vulnerability. People often think that a lot of wealth can protect them against the hazards of life and secure their future, but lessons from history show otherwise. Wealthy and influential people could not be shielded against death, nor against diseases. In present times, the world witnessed the death of many rich and powerful people during the COVID-19 pandemic, with their wealth being useless to help them!

---

[27] *A'yaan al-Shia*, Al-Ameen, vol. 3, pg. 617.

11

The Effects of Belief in Monotheism on Man's Life

لَّا تَجْعَلْ مَعَ ٱللَّهِ إِلَـٰهًا ءَاخَرَ فَتَقْعُدَ مَذْمُومًا مَّخْذُولًا

> Do not set up another deity along with God, lest you sit blameworthy, forsaken.[1]

[1] Qur'an, Surah al-Isra (17), verse 22.

The universe and everything in it cannot function without God's Guidance. It sustains and empowers all of humanity. Every success and prosperity that exists comes from and through God.

وَمَا بِكُم مِّن نِّعْمَةٍ فَمِنَ ٱللَّهِ

> And whatever blessing you have - it is from God.[1]

God, who is Omnipresent, Omnipotent, and Omniscient, can be reached in several ways. Though He is Transcendent, but yet Imminent, He is closer to us than our jugular vein. The signs that lead to Him are countless, and each individual can establish a relationship with God, according to one's own spiritual and mental capacity.

Direct and Indirect Connection with God

وَكُلُّ شَىْءٍ عِندَهُۥ بِمِقْدَارٍ ۝ عَٰلِمُ ٱلْغَيْبِ وَٱلشَّهَٰدَةِ ٱلْكَبِيرُ ٱلْمُتَعَالِ

> And everything with Him is according to a measure. Knower of the Unseen and the seen, the Great, the Exalted.[2]

Prophet Muhammad reiterated his need for God's help; and he repeatedly manifested to his community his dependence upon the Almighty One.

There are two types of God's intervention mentioned in the Qur'an: direct and indirect intervention. The first type speaks about God's direct intervention in our lives, without a human factor.

---

[1] Qur'an, Surah al-Nahl (16), verse 53.

[2] Qur'an, Surah al-Ra'd (13), verses 8-9.

وَلَقَدْ نَصَرَكُمُ ٱللَّهُ بِبَدْرٍ وَأَنتُمْ أَذِلَّةٌ ۖ فَٱتَّقُوا۟ ٱللَّهَ لَعَلَّكُمْ تَشْكُرُونَ

> And God certainly helped you at Badr when you were lowly. So have the reverence of God, that haply you may give thanks.[3]

وَأَنزَلَ جُنُودًا لَّمْ تَرَوْهَا

> And sent down (in the battle) hosts (angels) whom you did not see.[4]

The Qur'an states in these two verses that in fact, it was not the swords and armor that gave the Muslims victory in the battle of Badr; rather, victory was achieved by God's help and direct intervention, by sending down unseen angels when the Muslims were outnumbered by their enemies. This is an example of a direct intervention from God.

In other instances, God intervenes indirectly. This means that He provides help and assistance through man's initiative and actions. An example of this is:

وَأَعِدُّوا۟ لَهُم مَّا ٱسْتَطَعْتُم مِّن قُوَّةٍ وَمِن رِّبَاطِ ٱلْخَيْلِ تُرْهِبُونَ بِهِۦ عَدُوَّ ٱللَّهِ وَعَدُوَّكُمْ

> And prepare against them what you can of strength and horses tethered, frightening thereby the enemy of God and your enemy.[5]

---

[3] Qur'an, Surah Ale Imraan (3), verse 123.
[4] Qur'an, Surah al-Tawbah (9), verse 26.
[5] Qur'an, Surah al-Anfaal (8), verse 60.

Likewise, there are two types of links one can establish with one's Lord. One is a direct link, and the other one is indirect. A verse that speaks about a direct link with God is the following:

إِيَّاكَ نَعْبُدُ وَإِيَّاكَ نَسْتَعِينُ

> You (alone) do we worship, and from You (alone) do we seek help.[6]

This is when one speaks directly with God without any intermediaries.

At times, one seeks help from God through other legitimate means, and this is an indirect link with God.

وَٱسْتَعِينُوا۟ بِٱلصَّبْرِ وَٱلصَّلَوٰةِ

> And seek help through patience and prayer.[7]

Through the two acts of patience and prayer, one can establish an indirect link with God. In other words, these are means to get closer to Him. Patience in this verse is a reference to fasting. Though fasting appears to only be an abstention from food and drink, in fact it is a way of connecting one's self with God. Thus, the Qur'an states that the end result of fasting is to achieve God-consciousness and self-righteousness.

يَٰٓأَيُّهَا ٱلَّذِينَ ءَامَنُوا۟ كُتِبَ عَلَيْكُمُ ٱلصِّيَامُ كَمَا كُتِبَ عَلَى ٱلَّذِينَ مِن قَبْلِكُمْ لَعَلَّكُمْ تَتَّقُونَ

> O you who believe! Fasting is prescribed for you as it was prescribed for those before you, that perhaps you may be reverent.[8]

---

[6] Qur'an, Surah al-Fateha (1), verse 5.
[7] Qur'an, Surah al-Baqarah (2), verse 45.
[8] Qur'an, Surah al-Baqarah (2), verse 183.

Another way of achieving closeness to God is by helping each other through righteousness and kindness.

وَتَعَاوَنُواْ عَلَى ٱلْبِرِّ وَٱلتَّقْوَىٰ

> And help one another towards piety and reverence.[9]

One can also achieve closeness to God by speaking with kindness to other people, as this builds bridges of understanding and trust among individuals. These actions are indirect tools to help us get closer to God.

وَقُولُواْ لِلنَّاسِ حُسْنًا

> And speak to people in a good manner.[10]

Moreover, one can establish an indirect link to God, not only through working with believers and worshippers, but also with non-believers, if the intention is to spread peace and justice on Earth.

Dhul Qarnayn, one of the righteous men mentioned in the Qur'an, once asked a group of non-believers for assistance.

قَالَ مَا مَكَّنِّي فِيهِ رَبِّي خَيْرٌ فَأَعِينُونِي بِقُوَّةٍ أَجْعَلْ بَيْنَكُمْ وَبَيْنَهُمْ رَدْمًا

> He said: "That wherewith my Lord has established me is better; so aid me with strength. I shall set a rampart between you and them."[11]

Dhul Qarnayn helped the people of a village who could barely comprehend speech. The people did not worship God, but deserved to live in peace against their attackers, Gog and Magog.

---

[9] Qur'an, Surah al-Ma'idah (5), verse 2.
[10] Qur'an, Surah al-Baqarah (2), verse 83.
[11] Qur'an, Surah al-Kahf (18), verse 95.

Being non-worshippers did not deter Dhul Qarnayn from helping them achieve tranquility.

One may wonder: what is the role of God in a person's life when he encounters challenges and difficulties? Do prayers alone bring about a solution to these challenges, or are there other things that have to be done on man's side to overcome these trials? Responses to these questions follow in the next section.

Three Ways of Seeking Help

Seeking help can be through three main approaches.

1. The first way is seeking help by solely relying on God's miracles without making any effort from the person's side. Examples of this are praying to be rich without doing any work, praying for health without adopting a healthy lifestyle, or praying to be a learned person without actively acquiring knowledge. God does not desire us to have such attitudes. To not do anything on our part, but expect to have everything done for us, is defying all laws of cause and effect, and the laws of logic and intelligence. Of course, God is always there to help people who make an effort and endeavor to try their best.

2. The second way of seeking help is by only working hard and not asking God for any assistance. Someone who seeks wealth will work hard, and a person who is ill will get medical help. One might call this the material and practical way of seeking help, but they will not think it necessary to ask God for any intervention.

3. The third way of seeking help is a combination of the physical and metaphysical, or the material and the spiritual elements. Seeking help this way is done through praying to God, as well as working hard. This third way is the one which has been strongly encouraged in the Islamic tradition.

قُلْ مَا يَعْبَأُ بِكُمْ رَبِّي لَوْلَا دُعَاؤُكُمْ

> Say: "What weight would my Lord give you, were it not for your supplication?[12]

God is surely the best Helper and Sustainer for those who put in a serious effort in helping themselves. The Qur'an enforces this:

وَأَن لَّيْسَ لِلْإِنسَانِ إِلَّا مَا سَعَىٰ ۝ وَأَنَّ سَعْيَهُۥ سَوْفَ يُرَىٰ

> And that a person shall have naught except that for which one endeavors, and that his endeavoring shall be seen.[13]

It is imperative to rely on the natural means (working hard), alongside the supernatural means (prayers) to seek help. It is unwise to rely only on one and not the other, as this is against God's wisdom and contrary to what the Qur'an teaches us. God is the only effective power in this universe, but He still wants us to make an effort as well. One of the fundamental moral teachings of Islam is independence and self-reliance. One should always try his best to overcome challenges and hardships to achieve his goals. By surrendering to weaknesses and being inactive, no work can get done. God's message to man is that if he stands up and works hard, then God will back and support him whenever he needs help.

On the other hand, self-reliance and independence should not be a cause of arrogance or pride for man, for he still needs God's help, even if he does his work properly.

The history of the RMS Titanic serves as an example of the importance of relying on the material and spiritual means to seek help. It has been reported that the captain of the ship felt no need to say any prayers before the voyage, as he believed the ship to

---

[12] Qur'an, Surah al-Furqaan (25), verse 77.

[13] Qur'an, Surah al-Najm (53), verses 39-40.

be an unsinkable masterpiece. However, the Titanic ending up sinking because of human error, after it collided with an iceberg while on its maiden voyage from Southampton to New York. This "masterpiece" is now resting thousands of feet deep in the Atlantic Ocean.

It is essential that as human beings we understand our limits, because no matter how great a job one does, one is still limited in his abilities. Only God is completely limitless. Therefore, one should always ask Him for help and guidance in all of one's affairs, considering the limited minds and abilities of all human beings.

One of the recommendations of Islam is that when one travels, that along with logistic and technical preparations, one should pray to God to make the journey safe and hazardless. Spiritual connection with God provides people with energy, clarity, and self-confidence.

Spiritual Sustenance

One might wonder why a devout believer connects to God throughout the day and night. The answer to this is simply because of spiritual sustenance, just like a person needs to have several meals a day for physical sustenance.

يَٰٓأَيُّهَا ٱلَّذِينَ ءَامَنُوا۟ ٱذْكُرُوا۟ ٱللَّهَ ذِكْرًا كَثِيرًا ۝ وَسَبِّحُوهُ بُكْرَةً وَأَصِيلًا

> O you who believe! Remember God with frequent remembrance, And glorify Him morning and evening.[14]

Man needs God at all times or else one would not be able to handle the burdens of life on his own. When one knows that God

[14] Qur'an, Surah al-Ahzaab (33), verses 41-42.

is always there to take care of man, then the journey becomes less difficult because one knows that, ultimately, He is in charge of everything.

قَالَ لَا تَخَافَآ إِنَّنِي مَعَكُمَآ أَسْمَعُ وَأَرَىٰ

> He (God) said: "Fear not! Truly I am with you both; I hear and I see.[15]

When God told Prophet Moses and his brother Aaron to deliver His message to Pharaoh, He reassured them that He will be with them when they go to Egypt. Similarly, God is with other people too when they undertake a legitimate cause.

Everyone in this world needs a friend who will be there for them whenever they are needed. God is that real and true friend. He never abandons His servants. Praying five times a day is a reaffirmation that God is continuously watching over us, and He is with us in all of our affairs.

One need to hold on to the daily canonical prayers in order to avoid weakness and interruption in the journey of this life. When God was preparing His Messenger, Prophet Muhammad, for a strenuous mission to invite the pagans to Islam, He advised him to strengthen his relationship with his Lord during the midnight communion.

إِنَّا سَنُلْقِي عَلَيْكَ قَوْلًا ثَقِيلًا ۝ إِنَّ نَاشِئَةَ ٱلَّيْلِ هِيَ أَشَدُّ وَطْـًٔا وَأَقْوَمُ قِيلًا

> Truly We will soon cast upon you a weighty Word. Truly the vigil of the night is firmest in tread, and most upright for speech.[16]

---

[15] Qur'an, Surah Taha (20), verse 46.
[16] Qur'an, Surah al-Muzzammil (73), verses 5-6.

Midnight prayers (*Salat al-Layl*) are highly recommended for those who are seeking a higher level of spiritual refinement and a deeper connection with God. Through the offering of these special prayers, one can better navigate his way through this tumultuous life.

The Merit of Giving Thanks

What made Prophet Solomon a great king was not the vastness of his kingdom, but rather his humility before God. He knew that in the end, his kingdom was not his, and acknowledged that God is the ultimate Cherisher and Sustainer. Recognizing and giving thanks to God, Solomon prayed to Him for more opportunities to commit more acts of righteousness so he could be gathered with the righteous ones on the Day of Judgment.

وَقَالَ رَبِّ أَوْزِعْنِيٓ أَنْ أَشْكُرَ نِعْمَتَكَ ٱلَّتِيٓ أَنْعَمْتَ عَلَيَّ وَعَلَىٰ وَٰلِدَيَّ وَأَنْ أَعْمَلَ صَٰلِحًا تَرْضَىٰهُ وَأَدْخِلْنِي بِرَحْمَتِكَ فِي عِبَادِكَ ٱلصَّٰلِحِينَ

> And he (Prophet Solomon) said: "My Lord! Inspire me to give thanks for Your blessings which You have bestowed upon me and my parents, and to work righteousness (that is) pleasing to You; and cause me to enter, through Your Mercy, with Your righteous servants!"[17]

The more man gives thanks to God as the Cherisher and the Sustainer, the more one will be provided for. On the other hand, man should be careful not to be arrogant or ungrateful.

[17] Qur'an, Surah al-Naml (27), verse 19.

وَإِذْ تَأَذَّنَ رَبُّكُمْ لَئِن شَكَرْتُمْ لَأَزِيدَنَّكُمْ وَلَئِن كَفَرْتُمْ إِنَّ عَذَابِي لَشَدِيدٌ

> And when your Lord proclaimed: 'If you give thanks, then I will surely grant you increase (in favors); but if you are ungrateful, then indeed My Punishment is severe!'[18]

كُلُوا مِن رِّزْقِ رَبِّكُمْ وَاشْكُرُوا لَهُ

> Eat of the provision of your Lord and give thanks to Him.[19]

وَقَدِمْنَا إِلَىٰ مَا عَمِلُوا مِنْ عَمَلٍ فَجَعَلْنَاهُ هَبَاءً مَّنثُورًا

> And We shall turn whatever work they have done, and make it as scattered dust.[20]

The Qur'an stresses that any work which is done to obtain worldly gain rather than to seek the satisfaction of God, will lack devotion (*Ikhlaas*). Ultimately, the intention of a believer has to be to seek nearness to God, and have hope that one's actions will be accepted by Him.

God is always attentive to His creations' needs. It is people who need to reach out to Him, and try to benefit from His Mercy and Guidance.

وَإِذَا سَأَلَكَ عِبَادِي عَنِّي فَإِنِّي قَرِيبٌ أُجِيبُ دَعْوَةَ الدَّاعِ إِذَا دَعَانِ فَلْيَسْتَجِيبُوا لِي وَلْيُؤْمِنُوا بِي لَعَلَّهُمْ يَرْشُدُونَ

> And when My servants ask you about Me, Truly I am near. I answer the call of the supplicant when he calls upon Me.

[18] Qur'an, Surah Ibrahim (14), verse 7.
[19] Qur'an, Surah Saba (34), verse 15.
[20] Qur'an, Surah al-Furqaan (25), verse 23.

> So let them respond to Me and believe in Me, that they may be led aright.[21]

The Word "*Insha'Allah*" (God Willing)

Man should seeks guidance and direction from God in planning his future, not in isolation from Him. Man bears part of the responsibility in a good and wise planning for his life, and God bears the other part. Nothing can be done or should be planned without saying *insha'Allah* (God willing), since every plan needs to have God's permission before it is brought into action.

The term *insha'Allah* is an assertion of God's Power and Will over this universe. Many verses in the Qur'an refer to this fact, for example:

وَمَا تَشَآءُونَ إِلَّآ أَن يَشَآءَ ٱللَّهُ رَبُّ ٱلْعَٰلَمِينَ

> And you do not will except that God, Lord of the worlds, wills.[22]

وَلَا تَقُولَنَّ لِشَاْىْءٍ إِنِّى فَاعِلٌ ذَٰلِكَ غَدًا ۝ إِلَّآ أَن يَشَآءَ ٱللَّهُ

> And say not of anything: "Surely, I shall do it tomorrow," except that (one adds): "If God wills."[23]

قُل لَّآ أَمْلِكُ لِنَفْسِى ضَرًّا وَلَا نَفْعًا إِلَّا مَا شَآءَ ٱللَّهُ

> Say: "I have no power over what harm or benefit may come to me, except as God wills."[24]

If God does not permit for an event to take place, then no power in this universe can make that event happen. It is true that humans have a "free will," but this free will is not absolute, for if

---

[21] Qur'an, Surah al-Baqarah (2), verse 186.
[22] Qur'an, Surah al-Takweer (81), verse 29.
[23] Qur'an, Surah al-Kahf (18), verses 23-24.
[24] Qur'an, Surah Yunus (10), verse 49.

it was absolute, then it would have led to man's destruction. Nothing in this world is absolute, except for God. Oftentimes, one urgently presses for something to happen, but it does not happen because that specific event did not have God's permission to take place. When things do not go the way one wants them to, there is always a reason behind it. One might not know the reason until later on in life, or one may never even find out; but one must understand that God does not conduct His work arbitrarily. One must trust His Wisdom and Justice, and surrender to His will. Everything with Him is by due measure, because He is the Knower of the seen and the Unseen.

The word *insha'Allah* is important in the Islamic tradition, however unfortunately many take it lightly and use it loosely. People do not appreciate the significance and true meaning of this term.

12

Discovering God

أَفَلَا يَنظُرُونَ إِلَى ٱلْإِبِلِ كَيْفَ خُلِقَتْ ۝ وَإِلَى ٱلسَّمَآءِ كَيْفَ
رُفِعَتْ ۝ وَإِلَى ٱلْجِبَالِ كَيْفَ نُصِبَتْ ۝ وَإِلَى ٱلْأَرْضِ كَيْفَ
سُطِحَتْ ۝ فَذَكِّرْ إِنَّمَآ أَنتَ مُذَكِّرٌ ۝ لَّسْتَ عَلَيْهِم بِمُصَيْطِرٍ

> Do they not consider the camels, how they are created; the sky, how it is raised; the mountains, how they are established; and the earth, how it is spread? So remind (O Muhammad), you are but a reminder; you are not a warder over them.[1]

[1] Qur'an, Surah al-Ghaashiyah (88), verses 17-22.

Monotheism is Discovered through Intelligence

The concept of monotheism has been the foundation and stepping stone of all divine messages since the creation of man on Earth. It all started with monotheism, and connecting people to God.

In this life, man may enjoy a relationship with God, oneself, people, and the environment. Man has rights, duties, and responsibilities in every one of these relationships. The most important affiliation is man's relationship with God. God brought everyone into this world and sustains every single creation. Some people may express concern that they do not have enough sustenance to enjoy the luxuries of life. What they do not realize is that God has given them intelligence which, when used properly, can help them achieve some of the luxuries they crave for.

A narration from Imam Ali states:

> "Once Gabriel came to Adam and said: 'I am ordered to offer you three choices. You can choose one, and leave the other two.' Adam then asked: 'What are those three things?' Gabriel replied: 'They are intelligence, modesty, and religion.' Adam then said: 'I chose intelligence.' Gabriel then asked modesty and religion to return and leave intelligence with Adam; but they said to Gabriel: 'O Gabriel, we have been commanded to stay with intelligence wherever it exists.'"[1]

The most precious gift ever given by God to mankind is intelligence. If a person uses one's intelligence properly, then he will be able to achieve success and salvation. This is the reason why Islam, for example, strictly prohibits the use of destructive

---

[1] *Al-Kafi*, Book of Intelligence and Ignorance, Hadith 2, vol. 1, pg. 53.

substances, because they intoxicate the brain, and compromise a person's ability to think and act rationally.

When Prophet Joseph was wrongly accused for an act that he never committed and was imprisoned, he was patient and persevered. He shared his prison cell with two inmates who were polytheists. He said to them:

يَٰصَٰحِبَيِ ٱلسِّجۡنِ ءَأَرۡبَابٞ مُّتَفَرِّقُونَ خَيۡرٌ أَمِ ٱللَّهُ ٱلۡوَٰحِدُ ٱلۡقَهَّارُ

> O my two fellow prisoners! Are diverse lords better, or God, the One, the Paramount?[2]

مَا تَعۡبُدُونَ مِن دُونِهِۦٓ إِلَّآ أَسۡمَآءٗ سَمَّيۡتُمُوهَآ أَنتُمۡ وَءَابَآؤُكُم مَّآ أَنزَلَ ٱللَّهُ بِهَا مِن سُلۡطَٰنٍ

> You worship not apart from Him except but names that you have named - you and your fathers - for which God has sent down no authority.[3]

Prophet Joseph asked them this question so that they would answer it using their intelligence. By engaging in a conversation with them and letting them use their intelligence to give an answer, he invited them to monotheism.

Joseph argued that if multiple deities existed, then there would have been rivalries and conflicts between them, but this is not the case with a unified entity who brings everyone together under His order. This is exactly what monotheism means: submission to one unified entity who is not a dictator. God is All-Powerful, yet He is Just and Merciful. It is not God's Power that should be feared as being unjust, but man's power.

---

[2] Qur'an, Surah Yusuf (12), verse 39.
[3] Qur'an, Surah Yusuf (12), verse 40.

كَلَّآ إِنَّ ٱلْإِنسَـٰنَ لَيَطْغَىٰٓ ۝ أَن رَّءَاهُ ٱسْتَغْنَىٰٓ

> Nay, truly man is rebellious, In that he considers himself beyond need.[4]

Most people will become overcome with pride and arrogance once they are given any position of power. That is because humans are insufficient and limited in their abilities. God, on the other hand, is Self-Sufficient and does not require any recognition or fame. He does not need anyone or anything, while everyone and everything else needs Him.

It is imperative to realise that the best and easiest way to invite people to believe in God is through rational and intellectual discussions. Imam Muhammad al-Baqir states:

> When God created reason, He said to it: "I have not created anything more beloved to Me than you. It is you that I command, and you that I forbid, and through you that I will reward and punish."[5]

True leadership and guardianship in this universe belong to no one but God. If a person wishes to achieve internal satisfaction and success, then the only way to do so is to submit oneself completely to the will of God.

---

[4] Qur'an, Surah al-Alaq (96), verses 6-7.
[5] *Al-Kafi*, Book of Intelligence and Ignorance, Hadith 1, vol. 1, pg. 53.

Ways of Searching for God

قُلْ هَٰذِهِۦ سَبِيلِىٓ أَدْعُوٓا۟ إِلَى ٱللَّهِ ۚ عَلَىٰ بَصِيرَةٍ أَنَا۠ وَمَنِ ٱتَّبَعَنِى ۖ وَسُبْحَٰنَ ٱللَّهِ وَمَآ أَنَا۠ مِنَ ٱلْمُشْرِكِينَ

> Say: "This is my way. I call unto God with clear sight - I and those who follow me. Glory be to God! And I am not among those who ascribe partners to Him."[6]

It is critical that man stays true to the path he is following. However, how does a person know which path is the right one to follow? This is when intelligence is necessary. When it comes to following a religion, a person should do research, compare, and then see which one adheres to the truth the most.

بَلْ قَالُوٓا۟ إِنَّا وَجَدْنَآ ءَابَآءَنَا عَلَىٰٓ أُمَّةٍ وَإِنَّا عَلَىٰٓ ءَاثَٰرِهِم مُّهْتَدُونَ

> Nay! They say: "We found our fathers upon a creed, and surely we are rightly guided in their footsteps."[7]

To follow a certain religion merely because of one's ancestors or tribe, is not using one's intelligence. As mentioned previously, the greatest gift that God ever gave mankind is intelligence. To not utilize this gift properly is a complete waste and ungratefulness to God.

When it comes to religion, different theologians and philosophers believe that there are three ways to reach consciousness about God's existence: sense perception, intellectual inference, and spiritual intuition.

The first way to reach consciousness about God's existence is through "sense perception" - to depend on one's senses to reflect on His existence. God has made many signs, like the creation and

---

[6] Qur'an, Surah Yusuf (12), verse 108.
[7] Qur'an, Surah al-Zukhruf (43), verse 22.

functioning of the universe. Another great sign from God is the complex structure of the human body. Human beings live in bodies, yet have not mastered the knowledge about them. Every day mankind learns new things about the digestive system, the circulatory system, the respiratory system, the nervous system, and much more. Inside of the human body are major signs of God's wonders. The Qur'an has several verses about using one's intelligence to see God's signs.

إِنَّ فِي خَلْقِ ٱلسَّمَٰوَٰتِ وَٱلْأَرْضِ وَٱخْتِلَٰفِ ٱلَّيْلِ وَٱلنَّهَارِ لَءَايَٰتٍ لِّأُو۟لِى ٱلْأَلْبَٰبِ ۝ ٱلَّذِينَ يَذْكُرُونَ ٱللَّهَ قِيَٰمًا وَقُعُودًا وَعَلَىٰ جُنُوبِهِمْ وَيَتَفَكَّرُونَ فِي خَلْقِ ٱلسَّمَٰوَٰتِ وَٱلْأَرْضِ رَبَّنَا مَا خَلَقْتَ هَٰذَا بَٰطِلًا سُبْحَٰنَكَ فَقِنَا عَذَابَ ٱلنَّارِ

> Truly in the creation of the heavens and the earth, and the variation of the night and the day are signs for the possessors of intellect, who remember God while standing, sitting, and lying upon their sides, and reflect upon the creation of the heavens and the earth, (and say): "Our Lord, You did not create this in vain. Glory be to Thee! Shield us from the punishment of the Fire.[8]

وَفِي أَنفُسِكُمْ أَفَلَا تُبْصِرُونَ

> And within your souls. Do you not then see?[9]

The second way to reach consciousness about God's existence is through "intellectual inference." This way involves using one's intelligence to reflect on God's existence. The universe is a perfect system, and for such a perfect system to function, there

---

[8] Qur'an, Surah Ale Imraan (3), verses 190-191.
[9] Qur'an, Surah al-Dhaariyat (51), verse 21.

needs to be a perfect organizer. This organizer can only be God, as He is All-Perfect. A universe without God would completely collapse. It all comes down to asking a simple question: "Who created this universe?" If even a small country cannot function without a leader, then how can a vast universe function without God?

When it comes to finding God, one should always strive to find Him. Lacking the interest to search for Him will not bring Him to us.

"Spiritual intuition" is the third way to reach consciousness about God's existence. This is when a person's intuition leads one to God. Sometimes a lecture, a book, or a sermon is not what convinces an individual about the existence of God, rather one's own intuition does. This is because the spirit feels unfulfilled and is searching for a sense of fulfillment; it gets tired of artificial worldly affairs disguised as fulfillment, so it seeks for something real to fulfill its needs.

ٱلَّذِينَ ءَامَنُواْ وَتَطۡمَئِنُّ قُلُوبُهُم بِذِكۡرِ ٱللَّهِۗ أَلَا بِذِكۡرِ ٱللَّهِ تَطۡمَئِنُّ ٱلۡقُلُوبُ

> Those who believe and whose hearts are at peace in the remembrance of God. Are not hearts at peace in the remembrance of God?[10]

Upon discovering God, the human soul will thrive, because the void within will become filled with what it deserves. People with strong faith in God may survive with lack of materialistic needs, but it would be hard for them to do so without spiritual food, and even harder to survive without God. One of the most touching

[10] Qur'an, Surah al-Ra'd (13), verse 28.

stories of a strong bond between a human being with the Divine is the following:

> Once Prophet Jesus was walking with his disciples when he came upon a homeless man who was blind, crippled, and suffering from leprosy. Jesus asked this man about his condition. He replied: "Oh spirit of God, I am better than those whom God has not accorded them with what he accorded me with, and that is His recognition." Jesus asked this man about this best blessing. The man replied: "Even though I do not have vision, food, or shelter, I am rich on the inside, because I am well-connected with my Lord." Jesus turned to his disciples and told them that this is what real happiness looks like.[11]

We ask God to bestow upon us the ability and the opportunities to always be connected and attached to Him. We pray to be engrossed in His love, and only take Him as our true friend. For surely through doing so, will we be able to find complete salvation and true felicity.

---

[11] *Bihaar al-Anwaar*, Al-Majlisi, vol. 79, pg. 153.

Glossary of Terms

Abbas (ibn Abd al-Muttalib): The uncle of Prophet Muhammad, and although in the early days of Islam, he fought against the Prophet and Islam, later on his life, he converted to Islam and was a staunch supporter of the Prophet and Imam Ali.

Ahlulbayt: Lit. The family of the house - this honorific title is used multiple times in the Qur'an, however in Islam its usage is limited to specific family members of Prophet Muhammad - namely his daughter Fatima, her husband Ali, and their two sons, Hasan and Hussain.

Allah: The Arabic word for God.

Allahu Akbar: Lit. God is Greater than what He can be described with. A phrase which Muslims use to begin their daily prayers; it is also used frequently when a person wishes to extoll the greatness of God in one's daily life.

Al-Marwa: The second of the two mountains in the vicinity of the Ka'bah in Mecca which the pilgrims walk to and from during the minor (Umrah) and major (Hajj) pilgrimage.

Al-Safa: The first of the two mountains in the vicinity of the Ka'bah in Mecca which the pilgrims walk to and from during the minor (Umrah) and major (Hajj) pilgrimage.

Al-Tafweedh: The belief that God relegates some of His Responsibilities and Powers to certain beings as He chooses.

Al-Wilaayah al-Takwiniyyah: Lit. Constitutional Authority. The belief that God grants constitutional authority to certain beings as He chooses.

Al-Wilaayah al-Tashri'yyah: Lit. Legislative Authority. The belief that God grants legislative authority to certain beings as He chooses.

Angel Gabriel: The Angel who brought revelation to Prophet Muhammad - in Arabic, he is known as Jibraʾil.

Ash'arites (coercionists): Ashʿari theology, or Ashʿarism is one of the main Sunni schools of Islamic theology, founded by the Islamic scholar, Shafiʿi jurist, Sunni Muslim reformer and theologian Abu al-Hasan al-Ashʿari in the 10th century.

Awliyaah: Lit. The friends of God - this term refers to those who are not Prophets, Messengers, or Imams - but rather are devoted individuals of a high spiritual and religious calibre.

Azar: The uncle of Prophet Abraham who refused to accept the religion of his nephew.

Battle of Badr: The first battle fought in Islamic history which took place in 2 AH in which a small Muslim community fought against the polytheists of the Quraysh, winning an impressive win in the war by the help of God who sent angels to assist the Muslim army.

Black Stone: In Arabic, this is known as Hajr al-Aswad, and is the stone situated on one of the four corners of the Ka'bah which is encased in a silver bowl-like structure. Muslims try to touch it, or at least point towards it as they circumambulate the Ka'bah.

Dhul Qarnayn: An individual mentioned in chapter 18 of the Qur'an (Surah al-Kahf).

Ghuluw: To exceed the limits in ascribing ideas or Divine attributes to certain personalities of Islam that can only be ascribed to God.

Ibaadah: Lit. Worship of God.

Iblis: Satan, the devil. The first one to disobey God who refused to submit to the orders of God in a pre-worldly realm for which, he was banished to earth.

Ibn: Son of.

Ikhlaas: Lit. Sincerity, performing actions solely for the love and pleasure of God, and to seek spiritual proximity to Him.

Ilmul Ghaib: Lit. Knowledge of the Unseen. God has this entirely, and as per the necessary needs and requirements, He provides this Knowledge of the Unseen or future events to His select servants - namely Prophets, Messengers, and Imams.

Imam Ali: His full name is Ali the son of Abu Talib, and he is the cousin and son-in-law of Prophet Muhammad. He married the daughter of Prophet Muhammad, Fatima al-Zahra. For Shia Muslims, he is the first Imam - both spiritual and temporal leader, while for Sunni Muslims, he is the fourth caliph.

Imam al-Ridha: The eighth Shia Imam - his full name is Ali, son of Musa, and he bears the title of al-Ridha which means the content one.

Imam al-Sadiq: The sixth Shia Imam - his full name is Jafar, son of Muhammad, and he bears the title of al-Sadiq which means the truthful one.

Imam al-Zain al-Abedeen: The fourth Shia Imam - his full name is Ali, son of Hussain, and he bears the title of al-Sajjad which means the one who constantly prostrates to God.

Imam Hussain: The third Shia Imam - his full name is Hussain, son of Ali, and he bears the title of al-Shaheed which means the martyr - as he was martyred along with his companions and entire male family, with the exception of one of his sons and grandson, on the 10th of the Islamic lunar month of Muharram in Karbala in present day Iraq.

Intercession: The Qur'anic belief which states that on the Day of Judgment, God will permit certain individuals, such as the Prophets, Messengers, Imams, scholars, martyrs, and other select people, to intercede or advocate for people of their faith-tradition who may have committed sins in the life of this temporal world, however were not able to fully absolve themselves of those actions through the prescribed means such as asking forgiveness, paying a financial compensation, etc. These select people will ask God to absolve any remaining sins on their record, facilitating their entry into Paradise.

Israelites: The Tribes of Israel - the offspring of Prophet Jacob.

Jaʿfari School of Thought: The jurisprudential teachings which the Shia Ithna-Asheri exclusively follow are attributed to the sixth Shia Imam, Jaʿfar al-Sadiq, son of Muhammad, and thus are known as the Jaʿfari School of Thought.

Jinn: An unseen creation of God which exist in the same realm as human beings. They are of varying types just as humans: male and female, believer and non-believer.

Kaʿbah: The black square structure found in Mecca, Saudi Arabia in the Sacred Mosque; this is the direction which Muslims face towards for their five daily prayers.

Kufr: Lit. means to cover up. In terms of Islamic theology, it means to cover the truth and disregard God.

Mary: The virgin mother of Prophet Jesus - known in Arabic as Mariam. Chapter 19 of the Qur'an is named after her.

Mecca: A city in present-day Saudi Arabia which is famous for housing the Sacred Mosque in which the Kaʿbah is situation - the direction towards which all Muslims face for their daily prayers.

Mu'tazilites: Lit. 'Those who withdraw,' or 'Stand apart' - an ideology within Islam that appeared in early Islamic history in the dispute over Imam Ali's leadership of the Muslim community after the death of the third caliph, Uthman. Those who neither condemned, nor sanctioned Imam Ali or his opponents, but took a middle position between him and them in the battle of Siffeen and the battle of Jamal; these people were termed the Muʿtazila.

Pharaoh: The title for the king of ancient Egypt; in the Qur'an he is known as Firawn.

Prophet Abraham: Known in Arabic as Ibrahim, his story is narrated in multiple chapters of the Qur'an. He is the second of the five high-ranking Prophets of God.

Prophet Adam: The first Prophet sent by God to earth, who was accompanied by his wife, Eve (Hawwa).

Prophet David: Known in Arabic as Dawood, he was one of the Prophets sent to the Tribes of Israel.

Prophet Eber (Hud): Apparently, this Prophet of God is not mentioned in the Bible, although some dispute that he is the Prophet referred to as Eber in the Old Testament. He was sent to the community known as Aad.

Prophet Ishmael: Known in Arabic as Ismail, he was the first born son of Prophet Abraham to his slave-wife, Hagar (known in Arabic as Hajara). It is from his lineage that comes the final Messenger, Prophet Muhammad.

Prophet Jacob: Known in Arabic as Yaqoob, he had twelve sons including Prophet Joseph, and his extended family became known as the Tribes or Children of Israel.

Prophet Jesus: Known in Arabic as Isa, he was born from the virgin Mary (known in the Qur'an and Arabic as Maryam). He is the fourth of the five high-ranking Prophets of God.

Prophet John, the Baptist: Known in Arabic as Yahya, he was the first cousin of Mary (the mother of Prophet Jesus), and commenced his Prophethood in the era of Prophet Jesus and Prophet Zachariah.

Prophet Joseph: Known in Arabic as Yusuf, there is an entire chapter of the Qur'an named after him and his story of being separated from his family, sold into bondage, and eventually becoming the head of ancient Egypt.

Prophet Muhammad: The final Prophet that God sent for the guidance of humanity, he is the seal of the Prophets, and no

Prophet or Messenger will come after him. He is the fifth of the five high-ranking Prophets of God.

Prophet Moses: Known in Arabic as Musa. He is the Prophet who is mentioned the most in the Qur'an, and is the third of the five high-ranking Prophets of God.

Prophet Noah: Known in Arabic as Nuh. He is the first of the five high-ranking Prophets of God.

Prophet Saleh: Apparently he is not mentioned in the Bible, however he was a Prophet of God sent to the community of Thamud, and his story is recounted in many places of the Qur'an.

Prophet Soloman: Known in Arabic as Sulayman, he was one of the Prophets sent to the Children of Israel, and was the son of Prophet David.

Prophet Zachariah: Known in Arabic as Zakariyyah, he was married to the aunt of Mary, the mother of Jesus. His story, as well as his taking care of his niece, Mary, as she resided and worked in the temple, is recounted in the Qur'an in multiple instances.

Sahih al-Bukhari: One of the two canonical books of sayings attributed to Prophet Muhammad for Sunni Muslims. The Sunnis consider this book to be the most authentic book after the Qur'an.

Sahih Muslim: One of the two canonical books of sayings attributed to Prophet Muhammad for Sunni Muslims. The Sunnis consider this book to be the next most authentic book after the Qur'an and Sahih al-Bukhari.

Salat al-Layl: The night prayer - special recommended prayers that Muslims perform any time after midnight, but before the dawn prayer.

Satan: The devil.

Shafa'a: see Intercession.

Shirk: Lit. Polytheism - the act of associating partners with God in those areas which are strictly His domain of authority.

Station of Abraham: Known in Arabic as Maqam Ibrahim, this monument is contained within the Sacred Mosque of Mecca; it is a glass case which features the footprints of Prophet Abraham. Muslims are expected to perform a two-unit prayer behind this station after they complete their circumambulation of the Ka'bah.

Sunnah: Literally this means 'tradition' or 'way or custom' and most often when it is used, it refers to the way of life of Prophet Muhammad which Muslims are expected to emulate in their lives.

Tawheed: The Oneness and Uniqueness of God - He is One, has no partner, does not have any children, and Himself was not conceived or born into this world.

The Sacred Mosque: This refers to what is known in Arabic as Masjid al-Haraam, the sacred compound in the city of Mecca which houses the Ka'bah.

Umar ibn al-Khattab: The second caliph for the Sunni Muslims, and one of the father-in-laws of Prophet Muhammad.

Wali: An intimate servant of God.

Zamzam: A water-well in the city of Mecca which was first discovered by the wife of Prophet Abraham, Hagar, as she anxiously sought to find water for her young infant child, Ishmael.

Ziyaarah: Lit. Visitation - in Islamic terminology, it refers to the visitation to the resting site of anyone, however more specifically, the Prophets, Messengers, Imams, and other pious personalities.

Other Books by the Author

An American Muslim Preacher: Nuances of Islam in the West
BASED ON THE author's PhD dissertation for the International Colleges of Islamic Sciences in London, this work presents the outcome of over three decades of Islamic preaching and educational work in the West, and in particular, the United States of America. It spans the personal research and observations, as well as being supplemented with interviews conducted with various activists, scholars, educators, and academics in the United States - both men and women, Sunni and Shia. The contents include a study of the religious, social, and political identities of the American-Muslim landscape; the history and rise of Islam and Muslims in the United States, as well as the state of Islam and Muslims in contemporary America. The author also tackles the objectives, approaches, capabilities, and impediments of *da'wah* and *tabligh* in America, as well as the characteristics of a religious preacher in this context, and important topics of interfaith and intra-faith dialogue. The book closes with a summary of his own personal views and recommendations as it relates to educating others about Islam in North America.

Discovering Islam
A FRESH APPROACH to introducing Islam to the non-Muslim reader, this book introduces Islam by elaborating on the basic tenets of a faith which is practiced by over 1/6 of the world today. The author looks at the 'Pillars of Islam' - the theological beliefs upon which the faith is founded on, and then delves into the 'Roots of Islam' - the practices which the believers perform such as prayers, fasting, and almsgiving. The author also goes into an explanation of the various texts of Islam which the Muslims refer to for religious and spiritual guidance. This work ends with providing responses to contemporary questions asked

by non-believers concerning social life in Islam, human rights, women's rights, political activism, and other important topics.

Shia Islam

THIS WORK ATTEMPTS to bridge the gap between the Islamic schools of thought by clarifying common misconceptions about Shia Islam, and explaining philosophies and practices specific to the Shia school of thought. These issues are discussed primarily in the light of the Holy Qur'an, and the traditions of the Holy Prophet as related in the books of *hadith.* The prime goal of this book is to encourage true Muslim unity through dialogue to understand the different ideologies present in Islam today.

From Resolution to Revolution

A COLLECTION OF discussions focusing on the problems and challenges of the current era and solutions to counter them, this work is not just a transcript of 30 lectures delivered in the lunar month of Muharram; rather, it is also a thorough look at the human struggles and experiences which Muslims and non-Muslims face on a day-to-day basis. Although the words spoken and written are directed towards a youth audience, other readers will also benefit from this book by understanding the youth of our time. Their unique experiences and challenges in life require an equally unique approach to first define, then solve the social and religious issues that pertain exclusively to them.

When Power and Piety Collide

OVER FOURTEEN HUNDRED years have passed since Prophet Muhammad bonded rival tribes, united neighbors, and partnered the believers to form one community - the Muslim *ummah.* However, since the moment that the final Messenger publicly declared his Prophethood and message, the internal relationship of the Muslim *ummah* has yet to fully synthesize. Why is this so? In addition, how can a person better understand the fabric and tendencies of the Muslims? To understand the situation of the Muslims today, an objective and deep look into Islam's history and its key figures is critical. When Power and Piety Collide chronicles the early history of Islam, its development during the life of and shortly after the death of Prophet Muhammad, and then draws an illuminating light on the reasons why Muslims today have yet to establish a fully harmonious *ummah.*

Women - A New Perspective

A DIALOGUE THAT discusses and expounds upon the various issues regarding the rights and laws that pertain to women in Islam, and unwraps some of the distorted images and misconceptions that surround Muslim women. This work has been co-authored with Sister Fatma Saleh, with the various topics presented as a discussion.

Made in United States
North Haven, CT
16 July 2024